Hiram Fuller

Grand Transformation Scenes in the United States

Hiram Fuller

Grand Transformation Scenes in the United States

ISBN/EAN: 9783744678117

Printed in Europe, USA, Canada, Australia, Japan

Cover: Foto ©ninafisch / pixelio.de

More available books at **www.hansebooks.com**

GRAND TRANSFORMATION SCENES

IN

THE UNITED STATES

OR

GLIMPSES OF HOME AFTER THIRTEEN YEARS ABROAD.

BY

H. FULLER,

EDITOR OF THE COSMOPOLITAN;

Author of "*Belle Brittan's Letters,*" "*Sparks from a Locomotive,*"
"*North and South,*" "*The Flag of Truce,*"
"*The White Republican Papers*" in "*Fraser's Magazine,*"
&c. &c. &c.

NEW YORK:

G. W. Carleton & Co., Publishers.

LONDON: THE COSMOPOLITAN, 111 STRAND.

1875.

CONTENTS.

TRANSFORMATION SCENES.

	PAGE
THE VOYAGE	1
NEW YORK	6
POLITICS	13
FEDERAL UNION	20
HOTELS	27
BUSINESS	31
CHANGES	37
THE PARK	45
HEALTH	51
TRUTH	58
MONEY	64
CONGRESS	71
DOGS	80
THE BRANCH	88
THE COSMOPOLITAN	96
ELECTRICITY	105
GRANT	111
SARATOGA	116

	PAGE
BEECHER	128
PROVIDENCE	139
THE DRAMA	149

COSMOPOLITAN MISCELLANIES.

ENGLAND AND THE UNITED STATES	157
IF IT PLEASES THEM	167
THE POLICY OF INSURANCE	170
AMERICAN PRESS SCANDALS	173
INTERNATIONAL INHUMANITY	177
ROMANISM AND MASONRY	181
ENGLISH GIRLS IN LONDON	188
THE MARVELLOUS COUNTRY	191
END OF THE PRETENDER	199
THE DEVIL'S INVENTION	201
THE DREAMLAND OF THE PACIFIC	205
AMERICAN BONDS AND ENGLISH CONSOLS	211
STOCK EXCHANGE GAMBLERS	218
MONEY, BRAINS, AND MANNERS	223
THE BIRD	227
LIFE AMONG THE MODOCS	231
DISPOSAL OF DEAD BODIES	235
CHURCH AND THEATRE	239
THE SOLAR SYSTEM A SUCCESS	244

CONTENTS.

	PAGE
THE GILDED AGE	247
LIFE OF JOHN OF BARNEVELD	251
INDEPENDENT JOURNALISM	254
GERMAN OCTOPUS	257
PULLMAN ON THE MIDLAND	261
AMERICAN CENTENNIAL	268
EGYPT	271
COSMOPOLITAN ENTERPRISE	274
A RIGHTEOUS VERDICT	278
THE FUR COUNTRY	284
TALES OF THE STREET	289
LAW *v.* JUSTICE	291
A CHALLENGE TO JACK FROST	295
RETURN OF THE TIDAL WAVE	298
GOOD WISHES	304
DULCE DOMUM	309

THE VOYAGE.

On the 17th day of August 1861, leaning over the stern-rail of the steamship *Fulton*, I saw the last line of American land sink below the western horizon. On the 18th day of May 1874, at about two o'clock in the afternoon, peering from the upper deck of the steamship *Baltic*, I saw the same streak of land re-appear, after being lost to sight for nearly thirteen years. Within this long parenthesis of time many momentous things have happened, and many changes have taken place, both in the Old World and in the New, to say nothing of the changes we ourselves have undergone. But on these I do not propose to dwell. I commence this series of Transatlantic communications to *The Cosmopolitan*, not so much for the purpose of reviewing the past, as for describing the present condition, and, to some extent, forecasting the future, of the "reconstructed" Republic; and having heard so much from Americans abroad of the marvellous changes that have taken place in most of the cities of the North, and especially of the West, since the War, I was fully prepared to witness what I have deemed it no exaggeration to call "Transformation Scenes" in the United States. On walking last evening up Broadway, from Chambers Street to Union Square, I found the magic of the "Transformation" complete. This noble street, which for more than twenty years I daily traversed, in all seasons and at all times, did not present one familiar object. Was it a dream, or was it a new city? All the old landmarks are gone. The little shops have given place to immense "stores" and business palaces; while of the few old conservative mansions that for half a century stubbornly refused to "move up town" not one remained. The trees in the Parks are thirteen years taller, and even the flagstones on the sidewalks have more than doubled in size. Everything has grown, not only older and larger, but, paradoxical as it sounds, fresher and newer. At the "way things are going on," London will not change as much, materially, in the next hundred years as New York has changed in the last thirteen. But then London is pretty nearly "finished." It can continue to spread; but, in a certain sense, there is not much room for it to grow. The reader may pick an idea out of this "conundrum" if he can. To return to the ship. I must not pass lightly over what has brought me over so safely and so comfortably. The *Baltic*, of the White Star Line, is a splendid vessel. It is the only steamer on which I have never felt the jar of the machinery, nor smelt a "sea-sick" smell. Not a single pulsation or throb from her powerful engine is perceptible, while the atmosphere of the ship is absolutely inodorous. The table is better than that of most "first-class hotels," and the dining-room is almost as large as the Langham's. The coffee might and should be better; but this may be said of almost every public and even private table out of France. And there is no more excuse for vending bad coffee than for bad cigars. The best quality of both *can* be had, and Americans, of all people in the world, are willing to pay the price, as they are good judges of the article. Captain Kennedy, of the *Baltic*, is a "perfect brick," who minds his ship, and leaves his gallant doctors, purser, and steward, to look after the passengers. In a recent stormy passage he never left the bridge for three consecutive days and nights, having all his meals sent to him at his post. In "answering a fool according to his folly," Captain Kennedy is only equalled by the venerable Commodore Judkins. Captain Kennedy never drinks a drop of wine or spirits, and only occasionally comforts himself with a cigar or pipe. He gives you a curt "bob" on going on board, and an honest grip of the hand when you go on shore. And this is quite as much "attention" as passengers deserve from the captain. We were a little over eleven days in crossing, four of which were very rough, the balance of the time a pleasure-trip. Out of the one hundred so-called "first-class" passengers, there was about the average proportion of pleasant, companionable people, both ladies and gentlemen; and there was the usual tendency to flirtation. Only one case, however, became at all serious, threatening to end fatally—that is, in matrimony. One hoary old sinner made a fool of himself by entering two or three times the wrong state-room, which drew on him a sharp and well-deserved reprimand from the captain, and the general contempt of the indignantly virtuous passengers. But we had other incidents by the way, of a somewhat graver character, including a birth, a burial, and a christening. Among the seven hundred steerage passengers a Norwegian mother took it into her head to give birth to a boy; and as she was wholly unprepared for the event, and as the child was born utterly naked, we made up a purse of £5, by shilling contributions, to purchase a *layette* for the little nudity. And then, having a parson on board—

who, by the way, preached most inoffensive sermons, never obtruding his "stock-in-trade" upon the passengers—the baby was duly christened, to the great delight of several young matrons, one of whom acted as godmother. But ah! there was sadness on the sea when a little "steerage" boy of six died, and was dropped overboard. The ship's carpenter made the little coffin, added ninety pounds of weight to sink it, and, after early morning and burial prayers were read, there was a splash in the water, a gasp from the poor mother's heart, and the "funeral" was over. But there was such a mist that morning that many an eye could scarcely read the breakfast bill-of-fare. The path of life has its terrible passages, both on the land and on the sea.

NEW YORK.

THE Americans are an expansive people, and the reason is obvious. They are accustomed to rapid growth. The farmer is continually "pulling down his barns and building greater," and the merchant is perpetually enlarging his "stores." Business accommodations can hardly keep pace with the necessities of trade. Hence the magnitude and the splendour of those transformation scenes which meet the eye at every turn in the once-familiar city of New York. Broadway has no longer its cheap side, where the "lame ducks" used to sneak home after "bursting" in Wall Street. From the Battery all the way to Union Square, the noble thoroughfare is lined with magnificent business edifices, largely devoted to Banks, Insurance and Railway Companies. Oyster-cellars and confectionary saloons are no longer where they were, or what they were. Even bivalves and *bonbons* are now served in princely palaces; and wholesale clothing-shops have grown into huge establishments occupying entire blocks. Theatres have only multiplied, and not increased in size. But Barnum, the perennial and ever-expanding flower of showmen, has literally outgrown all competition and all tradition. In vastness, as in enterprise and audacity, Barnum beats the world. Between his old " Museum " on the corner of Ann Street and Broadway, and his new up-town " Hippodrome," there are whole centuries of progress. It is unquestionably the grandest and most bewildering " place of amusement " the world has ever seen. Just now it eclipses all other entertainments, and promises to be a great pecuniary success. The Roman Coliseum was but a mere hint to this " almighty spread " of the great showman in his fifth act. But in no class of buildings are the transformations more striking than in what used to be called newspaper " offices." In New York the Press has nobly asserted its dignity by the grandeur of its edifices. Instead of dirty, subterranean holes for press-rooms and publication offices, with miserable closets and garrets for editorial and composition rooms, all the first-class successful journals and magazines have risen, expanded, bloomed out, and become transformed into magnificent, regal-looking buildings, endowed with all modern improvements and luxuries in the way of light, warmth, ventilation,

&c., &c. Even the traditional "printer's devil" has been cared for in these "reconstructed" establishments, and water, soap, and towels supplied *ad libitum* for the benefit of his inky face and fingers. In fact, the dirty little imp of the newspaper office no longer exists. As for King Editor's throne-room, it is simply sumptuous. Sofas, easy-chairs—with *the* chair appropriately *on a pivot*—elegant cases filled with books of reference, speaking-tubes, electric bells, telegraph instruments, &c., &c., are all provided for the use of His Potency who commands the columns and assumes the imperial "We" of the Daily Press of New York. Something of a transformation this, since Bennet began to write his "shocking" leaders thirty-five years ago, with a cellar for his "sanctum," a board, resting upon two empty barrels, for a table, and a three-legged stool for his editorial chair. The *Herald* is now issued from a marble palace, and the son of the founder, whose birth was the text for a witty leader written by the happy father, headed, "Arrival of le Jeune Editeur," is now Prince of the Press, with a fortune of ten millions of dollars, more or less. These changes are truly amazing, and the more I see of what has been done here in the last thirteen years, the more convinced I am of the propriety of heading these observations—"Transformation Scenes." And, as yet, I have seen comparatively nothing. This is my fourth day in New York, and most of the time I have been immersed in Turkish Baths, of which I shall have more to say hereafter. The good doctor who presides over this beneficent institution assures me that he is saving me from a severe, if not fatal, case of cerebral and gastric fever, and that in ten days he will send me forth completely "reconstructed." The event of the day, or rather of yesterday, is the "Royal Marriage" at Washington. Miss Nellie Grant, daughter of the President, was married on the 21st inst., with most undemocratic pomp and ceremony, to Mr Sartoris, an Englishman, and the "happy pair" will depart to-morrow in the good ship *Baltic* for England. The leading journals of New York, with their customary competitive "enterprise," devote from six to eight columns to the joyful event. Truly the "Republican Court" has its courtiers, not to say toadies. To the parties immediately concerned in the "contract," this marriage of the Princess of the White House is of just as much importance as the marriage of the Grand Duchess of Russia to a son of the Queen of England; but, as a public or political event, it is hardly deserving of the ink that has been shed over it. Still it is better to throw " slippers " and bouquets after the "bridled pair" than anything that might hit harder or hurt more. And so let us join in the general *bon voyage* that wafts the beautiful *Baltic* on her homeward trip. Another feather in the " White Star's " cap—that is, Cap. Kennedy's, who has had his office on deck transformed for the occasion into a nuptial bower, but alas! not warranted proof against sea-sickness. And this reminds us of a philosophical conclusion very deliberately formed during our recent " crossing." A couple seriously inclined to marry should make a trip together across the Atlantic *before* the inexorable knot is tied. If both parties can stand the disillusionising effects of sea-sickness, they will have a better chance of sticking together through life. As I am again back in the ship—I don't mean that I am "going back on" the White Star Line—I am reminded of a touch of the Custom-House plague on landing. A friend, and a free-trader, who did not need this "protection" persecution to convert him to the true gospel of Commerce, was compelled to pay 288 dollars as "duties" on a few presents he was taking home to his family; while I was punished to the extent of twelve dollars on a little parcel which I had " the kindness to take " from a gentleman for his sister. Let me repeat for the thousandth time, and with renewed emphasis, that pro-

tection is a fraud, and the Custom House a nuisance.
The only honest and legitimate tax for the support of Government is a direct tax on property.
One word in regard to business matters. Trade
is dull, and bankers are blue. Wall Street
"operators" tell me they are not making their
rents. Only that accursed "Gold Room," the
great Gambling Hell of New York, keeps up the
game of buying and selling at fluctuations of an
eighth or a sixteenth a day, by which one wins a
little, another loses, and nobody is benefited. I
am looking into "Erie," and shall soon be able
to report as thoroughly on the affairs of the
Company as Captain Tyler, the outcoming man.
I will only say to-day that the Erie will lease the
Atlantic and Great Western for ninety-nine years,
that President Watson will retire, and that Mr
James McHenry will return to England next
week perfectly satisfied with matters and things
generally. Mr McHenry is regarded here as the
reigning "Railway King" of America. On leaving this week for a trip to Niagara, the venerable
Commodore Vanderbilt met him at the station
at an early hour in the morning, and placed a
Palace Car at his service. The Commodore has
passed his eightieth year, and still loves his big
stock game in Wall Street, and his little game
of "Boston" at the club. When this old man's

many-wintered snow melts, there will come a deluge. The wealth now dammed up in that weak old reservoir is stupendous; and in this case the transformation scene cannot be long delayed.

POLITICS.

POLITICAL changes in America transcend even material transformations. Within a decade Negro Slavery in the South has been abolished, and the once " Sovereign and Independent States " have been deprived of all their original " rights." This radical revolution is the result of the great Secession War, which has left society, and the " body politic," in a very unsettled condition. When the negroes were suddenly emancipated by the accident of Northern victory, the Federal Congress, in which the Southern States had no representative, bestowed on the " freedman " the privilege of citizenship, thereby conferring on the ignorant blacks of the South the balance of political power. Time will illustrate the folly of this indiscriminate enfranchisement. Already it has introduced a new word to the criminal vocabulary; and " carpet-baggism " is the acknowledged curse of the country. It has brought upon the subjugated South more debt than the Rebellion, and more disgrace than Secession. No sooner had the Act passed Congress, giving to all negroes of the age of twenty-one the right to vote, than a hungry horde of political adventurers, carpet-bag in hand, rushed down South to "take charge of the elections." Calling themselves "Original Abolitionists" they assumed to be the negro's friend and liberator, and of course had things all their own way. Getting control of the local Legislatures, they soon feathered their own nests by issuing State Bonds without limit and without record. Hence the hopeless bankruptcy of most of the "States lately in rebellion." South Carolina is being sold by Sheriffs to pay the taxes on these fraudulent bonds. These observations are *apropos* of the so-called "Civil Rights Bill," which has just passed the Senate at Washington by a strictly party vote, only three Republicans having the courage to protest against the monstrous measure. This "Bill" is Mr Sumner's dying legacy—I will call it insult—to his country. The following "First Clause" contains its principal "provisions." The rest of the Act is made up chiefly of pains and penalties for violation of this preposterous and most offensive law:—"That all citizens and other persons within the jurisdiction of the United States shall be entitled to the full and equal enjoyment of the accommodations, advantages, facilities, and privileges of inns, public conveyances on land or water, theatres and other places of public amusement, and also of common schools and public institutions of learning and benevolence supported in whole or in part by general taxation, and of cemeteries so supported, and also the institutions known as agricultural colleges, endowed by the United States, subject only to the conditions and limitations established by law, and applicable alike to citizens of every race and colour, regardless of any previous condition of servitude." The *New York Herald* of the 24th of May has an able and justly indignant leader on the subject, from which I quote the following pithy extract:—" In the first section of this Bill for Civil Rights, Congress pretends to lay down rules for the hotel-keepers, to say who shall travel in public conveyances, and to govern the theatres and places of amusement generally to legislate for our common schools, colleges, hospitals, insane asylums, and charitable institutions generally ; nay, even to declare who shall be buried in our potters' fields—for we believe those are the only graveyards we have that are not private property. Further than all this, Congress proceeds to declare who shall sit on the grand juries in the several States, who shall serve as petit jurors, and to lay down penalties for the misconduct of the Commissioners of Juries and similar strictly local officials. All this is not merely unconstitutional, it is absurd and nonsensical. It does not merely transcend the power of Congress, but it goes beyond the point up to which people can contemplate the law with respect, and, at least, with straight faces." This reckless party Act sweeps away the last vestige of State Rights, and utterly extinguishes State autonomy. Will the House pass it? and if so, will the President sanction it? are the questions on every tongue. It is vain to predict what time will so soon decide; but the chances are all in favour of this measure of nonsense becoming the supreme law of the land. In the first place, it is a strictly party measure, and the party has a large majority in the House. This secures the passage of the Bill. And there is not the slightest hope for a veto from Grant, who is beyond doubt again in the field for re-election. It is now said that men seeking favours at the White House must either mollify Grant with the prospect of a third term, or menace him with impeachment. Therefore he will not veto the Bill which makes the negro, *perforce*, the social equal of the white man, as the negro vote controls the South, and is the balance of power in the Presidential election. Only two primary laws govern the Universe—

gravitation and self-interest. It is the interest of Presidential aspirants to truckle to niggerdom. Having weakened himself in the West and South by his brave veto of "Inflation," Grant will now hedge on the niggers. Lest some casual reader of the *Cosmopolitan* should misinterpret my views in regard to the social and political *status* of "our coloured brethren," I will here state that, while naturally and honestly preferring white skins to black, I would *not* disfranchise a man for the mere accident of colour: I would only restrict the privilege of suffrage to men who possess the requisite moral, intellectual, and property qualifications. On the firm basis of *equal* suffrage Republics may endure for centuries; but on the rotten foundation of *universal* suffrage the inevitable downfall is only a question of time. As a race the African is in its nonage, and not half as much entitled to vote as the average white boy of twelve. Under the illogical "Fourteenth Amendment" to the Federal Constitution every American white man, less than twenty-one years of age, is every black man's political inferior; and now the "Civil Rights" enactment makes the very lowest darkey the social equal of the very highest white. When the President has put his name to this infamous law, the most offensive nigger, in the hottest of the dog-days, can demand a seat at the *table d'hôte* of the most aristocratic hotel, and the refusal of his demand, or the ejectment of his person, would subject the hotel-keeper to a fine of 1000 dollars. The effect of this enforced association, in violation of the great law of " natural selection," will be a war of races, and the final extirpation of the blacks. And yet the New York *Tribune* says the law is but the enactment of the Golden Rule, and that Sumner, like the Campeador, has gained his greatest victory after death! As I have already intimated, Grant, playing for a third term, will sign the Bill. One word in regard to this much deprecated third-term movement. What is the particular objection to it? There is no precedent for it, the Opposition newspapers daily iterate. True, but there is no precedent for many things that have been done in Washington since the Black Republican party came into power in 1861. And if the President is a good one, and his administration is beneficent, the longer he remains in office the better. Only, let him be elected for a longer term—say ten or twelve years, or even for life—to avoid the demoralising effects of quadrennial elections. There is no better reason than precedent for not electing the Chief Magistrate, like the Judges of the Supreme Court, for life, instead of four years.

Given a good Executive, and the longer he remains in office the better will he be qualified to discharge its duties. Therefore we see no insuperable objection to a third term for Grant. He has been tried, and the people have confidence in the general policy of his administration. There is a homely old proverb applicable to the situation—" One may go farther and fare worse." Sporting politicians are now betting that the only possible alternatives for the next Presidency are Grant and Butler. The mere menace is rapidly reconciling thousands to the idea of a third term.

FEDERAL UNION.

SINCE my arrival in New York a new State has been added to the Federal Union. To the general surprise of the public, the Territory of New Mexico comes in ahead of Colorado, as number thirty-eight. After a somewhat animated debate, the Bill of Admission passed the Lower House by a vote of 160 to 76. It was stated in the course of the discussion that New Mexico, which has an area three times as large as Ohio, had in 1850 a population of 61,547, and in 1860 a population of 93,516. But in 1870 the advocates of the Bill were forced to admit there had been, according to the census, an actual decrease, for the population was then shown to be only 91,971. The decrease was declared to be "apparent" only, and Mr Elkins, the delegate from New Mexico, devoted much of his time to explaining it away. He asserted that the present population is at least 135,000, and he showed that fifteen of the twenty-four States admitted since the original thirteen had an average population of 63,000 at the date of admission. The geographical position and agricultural and mineral resources of the infant State are already exciting a lively interest. The population is chiefly Mexican, and the business of the Territorial Legislature has been carried on through an interpreter. Great progress has been made within the last five years, no less than 133 public schools having been established, and the mineral productions have risen to over 2,000,000 dollars a year. A Bill admitting Colorado into the Union has just passed the Territorial Committee of the House of Representatives, and before Congress adjourns on the 22d of June the Federation will consist of thirty-nine States, just three times the original number. The only valid ground of opposition to the admission of new States is the undeserved power it gives them in the Senate. On the next meeting of Congress, New Mexico, which has two senators, will have just as much voting strength in the Upper House as New York. Considering that the population of the former is only a little over 100,000, most of whom can neither read, write, nor *speak* the English language, while the latter numbers about 5,000,000, embracing the most intelligent and wealthy citizens of the Union, the injustice of the Constitutional " provision " becomes strikingly apparent.

But so long as the law exists, Territories have the absolute right of admission whenever they can show the requisite number of inhabitants, including Niggers, Indians, Mexicans, hybrids, and all other bipeds belonging to the genus *homo*. It is given out that before 1876, the Centennial Birthday of the great Republic, the Federal Union will consist of forty States, and the Senate of eighty members. To check this rapid increase of States an "amendment" may possibly be passed raising the population standard to 500,000 or 1,000,000. Congress has long since ceased to regard the Constitution as an instrument too sacred to be altered, amended, or even violated. At this very moment a Washington telegram brings us the following proposition, introduced to the Senate by Mr Stewart, of Nevada, in the shape of a Sixteenth Amendment:—"Article 16: If any State shall fail to maintain a common school system, under which all persons between the ages of five and eighteen years, not incapacitated for the same, shall receive, free of charge, such elementary education as Congress may prescribe, the Congress shall have power to establish therein such a system, and cause the same to be maintained at the expense of such State." Anything in favour of public education is sure to meet the general approbation of the American people; but this

Amendment is another blow at State Rights, of which the less said hereafter the better. The very phrase sounds like burlesque, and reminds one of the ironical Yankee shoemaker who advertises "Women's Rights and Lefts." In the eye of Congress—that is, of the dominant party—the individual States, once "sovereign and independent," are reduced to mere municipalities, and their respective Legislatures might as well be abolished, and all the "State-Houses" converted into school-houses or Turkish-bath establishments. Here is a transformation, indeed, since the good old days when Massachusetts and South Carolina held their heads high and defiant—one the first to threaten Secession through a "Hartford Convention," and the other to inaugurate the "Sovereign" idea by an attack on Fort Sumter. Is it possible that the spirits of Webster and Hayne are cognisant of the present condition of these proud old States, of which, a brief generation ago, they were the respective and eloquent champions? I am here reminded of certain questions frequently asked in Europe. Has the general condition of the American people been improved by the war? Has the emancipation of the blacks increased the liberty of the whites? Have a few gigantic shoddy fortunes benefited the masses of the people? All these questions I must answer emphatically in the negative. War is the sum of all crime, and its fruits are only evil. And there never was a more wicked war waged on earth than the great fratricidal war between the North and the South. But it is past, and I do not propose to discuss it, only to " cuss it" now and for ever. As for apportioning the blame among parties, sections, and individuals who brought the Red Deluge upon the country, *that* is a matter for the Court of Last Appeal, before whom, according to orthodox creed, all motives and men must be finally judged and sentenced. As my pen runs in a political vein today, it catches somewhat eagerly at the Cuban news of recent date. There is a great pressure on Congress at this moment for the official recognition of the "patriots" as belligerents. A leading article in the *Cosmopolitan* of the 7th of May, *apropos* of Senator Carpenter's Recognition Motion, was conspicuously quoted by the Washington *Chronicle*, the organ of the Administration. This prominent indication of Presidential support gave the friends of Cuba renewed hope, and they have gone to work in earnest to induce Congress to act before adjournment. It is a singular fact that the New York *Times*, the organ of Secretary Fish, is very angry at the Cuban movement, and calls on the Government to repudiate the course of the *Chronicle*, whose editor is grossly abused for his "sympathies." But the *Times* is edited by an Englishman, who has the impudence, in his issue of this morning, to blackguard the venerable and respectable Mayor Havemeyer in the following words, and for the simple reason that the Mayor has signed the ordinance for muzzling dogs:— "We have known many a dog far more intelligent, and far more fit to be Mayor of New York, than Mr Havemeyer—and doubtless not a few of our readers can say the same." Suppose an American journalist in London should write thus insolently of the Lord Mayor! The Spanish despotism in Cuba is really helping the cause of the "patriots" more effectively than all the sympathies at Washington. Here is an item that touches the Americans in a tender spot:—A letter from Havana, of the 22d of May, says that the "merchants exporting goods to the United States from Cuba are already adding the income-tax of ten per cent. levied by General Concha to the invoices which they remit to their correspondents in the United States. The plan is exceedingly simple on their part, takes no money out of their pockets, nor out of those of the people of the island —the people of the United States thus almost directly paying the income-tax of the Cubans." This one little fact will do more to bring about the recognition of the Cuban Republic than all other causes combined. Brother Jonathan is a sensible fellow, and most "sensible" of all in his pocket. Just now there is a general complaint of stagnation in business. The bankers are blue, and railroad men are "far, far from gay." New York has too many magnificent stores to let. The merchants wear long and anxious as well as meagre faces. The recognition of Cuba will create a new sensation, and make things lively generally. Mr Secretary Fish fears a war with Spain. None but old fogies are afraid of ghosts. Spain has her hands full of war at home. It would be a positive blessing to the Mother Country to get rid of her Cuban troubles. But the question for the United States to consider is, not the pleasure or pride of Spain, nor one of mere commercial benefits to herself and to the world at large, but a question of human freedom and of human right. A people who appeal to "higher laws" whenever it suits their interests to override the Constitution, should not hesitate to act under the same code when the cause of human liberty is at stake. In spite of the powerful Spanish influence in Washington, chiefly exercised through the office of the Secretary of State, or Prime Minister, I have strong assurances from headquarters that the hour of Cuban deliverance is at hand.

HOTELS.

THERE has been a large increase in the number of hotels in New York in the last ten years, but the rage for " mammoth hotels " no longer exists. The ambition for magnitude seems to have culminated in the " St Nicholas," and the " Fifth Avenue." Hotels about one-half the size of these enormous establishments are now considered quite as comfortable, and even more fashionable. A few years ago American travellers, both at home and abroad, thought it a "big thing," and the only " correct thing," to stop at the " biggest house." But European ideas, which are continually modifying " Yankee notions," have corrected the popular fallacy that a man's personal importance depends on the magnitude or the magnificence of his domicile. After making acquaintance with the big town of London, the great reservoir of wealth and hotbed of aristocracy, the American loses something of his worship of vastness, and comes to the conclusion that quality is even more desirable than quantity.

A small diamond is worth more than a big rock, and a single drop of "attar" than a whole acre of roses. Among the hotel guests of London we generally find the most fastidious and "exclusive" visitants at such "one-horse concerns" as Long's, Limmer's, Claridge's, and Fenton's, rather than at those very grand hotels, the Langham, the Grosvenor, the Charing Cross, and the Midland. This "fashion" has reached New York, which is sufficiently cosmopolitan to adopt good ideas from abroad, even if they come from England. There are several comparatively small hotels up town kept on the "European plan," which come about as near to perfection in the way of comfort as any hotels I have seen in any part of the world. They have a fixed price for rooms, and the meals are served *à la carte;* the cost of every dish is given, so that no one need be surprised or vexed at the amount of his bill. In the United States the hotel is literally an "institution." The system, initiated here some forty years ago, has revolutionised the hotel system throughout the world. I can give its origin by indulging in a little egotism. At the age of twelve, in passing through Boston, on my way to school at Newhampton, N.H., I had to pass a night at the Tremont House, then newly opened, which was the first "grand hotel" ever built in America, or in Europe. Behind the office counter of that hotel I saw a remarkably handsome boy, about my own age, who was affectionately called "Charley." A few years later this promising lad, Charles A. Stetson, in connection with Robert B. Coleman, became proprietor of the Astor House in New York, then the "mammoth hotel" of the world. During my first year's residence in New York, as Editor of the *Evening Mirror*, it was my good fortune to be a guest at the Astor. Last week, in the vestibule of the Astor, I met my old friend, and sometime host, Stetson. We are both not a little metamorphosed by Time, but have not lost our identity. *We recognised each other.* While on the subject of hotels, I have an important announcement to make. My good old friend Hiram Cranston, at whose beautiful country seat, 150 miles north of New York, I am now writing, proposes to build the grandest hotel in London the world has ever seen. His drawings, put in shape by Arthur Gilman, the celebrated architect, give us an ideal hotel. The "Grand," in Paris, where I have resided for four years, and which I used to think was, in every respect, the *ne plus ultra* of hotels, is simply "nowhere" in comparison with these plans, which have cost Mr Cranston some ten thousand dollars. I shall not undertake to describe them. I only hope the old Coliseum lot, fronting Regent's Park, can be obtained for the erection of this super-grand hotel, the embodiment of Mr Cranston's idea. Is there room for another grand hotel in London, I am asked? My answer to this is a practical one. The Langham, which pays 18 per cent. dividends, is turning away hundreds daily. And the Langham does not give its American guests an "American Bar," nor American dishes—corn bread, hominy, cod-fish balls, buckwheat cakes, pickled oysters, succotash, &c. Yes, there is not only room for, but a great want of, an American hotel in London; that is, not an exclusively American hotel, but one in which both the English and American systems are combined; and this Mr Cranston, who is acknowledged to be the king of American hotel-directors, proposes to do. I have heard several parties of "elegant leisure" say, "If Cranston opens a hotel in London, we will go there to spend the remainder of our days." Let Cranston, of the famous "New York," and Curtis, of the excellent "Limmer's," unite their "experiences," and London will have such a hotel as the world has never seen.

BUSINESS.

Business affairs in New York are reposing in a salutary state of inactivity. This is the effect of the last September panic. So many bankers and railway speculators of the paper millionaire class were suddenly jerked up and laid on their backs, that retrenchment and economy have become the fashion of the day. Diamond studs have vanished from the shirts of Fifth Avenue "swells," and now scintillate chiefly on the "fronts" and fingers of nigger minstrels. Spreading and splurging, to use vernacular phrases, are played out, and there is little ambition to do a fictitious business. The building trade is almost at a standstill, and there are many magnificent stores to let in the most active business streets of the city. Dealers in bonds, shares, and promises to pay of every description, are all droning the same dull tune— "Nothing doing." And yet I regard this state of suspended animation, popularly called "stagnation of trade," as one of the most healthful signs of the times. The simple truth is, the Americans, and particularly the New Yorkers, were going ahead too fast, on the delusive current of paper money. Everything after the war was *couleur de rose*. Everybody was expansive, and everything inflated. The multiplication of banks, the increase of railroads, and the unlimited issues of the Federal Treasury, inundated the community with a "circulating medium" that passed for money, and which, piled up in the banker's safe, was regarded as actual wealth. When the panic came, beginning with the collapse of Jay Cooke & Co., the great Government banking-house, these redundant promises to pay suddenly shrivelled, and were of no more avail than "filthy rags." Wall Street dealers in "paper" instantly lost confidence in their own "stock-in-trade," and more especially in each other. The effects of this wholesome check are now apparent in the utter absence of the usual spirit of speculation, and in what is called the "deadness of the street." In the mercantile world there is more life. The average weekly exports from New York exceed 5,000,000 of dollars, and this alone involves a good deal of business; while the imports are considerably less than this amount—an excellent indication for the prosperity of the future, and that too not a remote future. The business world of New York may reasonably look for a great revival of trade in the autumn. In the mean time, economy, following in the wake of extravagance, like Ruth gleaning in the field of Boaz, is daily making the people richer, and thousands who have been for years living beyond their legitimate incomes are now struggling to live within them—the only sure way to domestic comfort and pecuniary independence. Emigration from Europe is adding enormously to the aggregate wealth of the country. An average of one thousand a day of imported "citizens" continue to land at Castle Garden, and straggle through New York on their sad yet hopeful way to the unlimited West, where "there's bread and work for all." In spite of illogical legislation and corrupt officials—in spite of the great fraud of a protective tariff, there is no reason to croak over future bankruptcy or popular repudiation in the United States. It is true, the aggregate debt of Federal, State, and City Governments, to say nothing of Railway corporations, and merchants' outstanding bills, is enough to make one's head swim; but there is always to be taken into account a set-off in the unlimited resources of the country to meet this Olympian obligation. Within five years from this date the United States will almost cease to be importers of Iron and Wine, and become large exporters of these costly commodities. The same will be true, in a great degree, of Coffee, Tea, and Silk. Within five years, also, railways built with European capital, many of which are now in a very unsatisfactory pecuniary condition, will be able to pay dividends and divide bonuses on their shares. These are not mere sanguine prophecies, but simple mathematical calculations based on positive facts. Take the *ratio* of increase at the most moderate figure, and cipher out the results. *Apropos* of railways, I am aware that many European readers of the *Cosmopolitan* are anxiously waiting to hear something positive and reliable in regard to the "state of Erie." This information I am diligently seeking, quite independently of Captain Tyler, and the brace of London accountants, who are just now up to their eyes in the Erie books. But I am not prepared to report to-day. Immediately on my arrival in New York, two weeks ago, I wrote that Mr Watson would resign his position as President of the Company. To-day this item of "news" appears, with comments, in all the daily papers. There is a grand "operation" going on between the Erie and the Atlantic and Great Western, which it was the object of Mr McHenry's visit here to initiate, and which he has gone back to London to consummate by obtaining the assent of the shareholders. Mr McHenry is regarded here as "master of the situation." Combining his indomitable energies and great financial abilities with such "Powers" as Commodore Vanderbilt and Colonel Tom Scott, who has just been elected President of the Pennsylvanian Road, and with whom he is in cordial and active alliance, Mr McHenry has the game all in his own hands. These three vast railway consolidations, controlled by McHenry, Vanderbilt, and Scott, represent a capital of over 500,000,000 of dollars! I fully believe this entire investment will ultimately average a twenty per cent. dividend. All that these great American enterprises want is time and confidence to pay splendidly. We have news here to-day of the arrival of the Faraday at Nova Scotia with the new Direct Cable *on board*. Everybody is asking—Why was it not laid in coming across? Are they going to begin on this side to pay out? A telegram has just come in announcing that the shore-end is being laid from Nova Scotia to Rye Beach, New Hampshire, and there are vague mutterings from Washington that Mr Secretary Fish will not allow the cable to land. How is this? The English Company bought the right to land, conceded by Congress in 1867 to Mr Cornell Jewett and his associates, and surely Mr Fish will not undertake to annul the Act of Congress! The public need not be surprised to learn that this threatened interference on the part of the Government may be used as a sort of thumbscrew to force the " Direct Cable Company " to sell out to the old monopoly. And thus our dream of cheap cablegrams may again be disappointed. But we have still another hope, a well-grounded one, for the fulfilment of this most desirable object: Van Choate's Atlantic Cable Company is formed, with the requisite concessions from no less than five European Governments, and the capital to lay it (£2,500,000) is already raised.

CHANGES.

A few remarkable instances of individual transformations rise before me to-day. I will mention no names, as the features will be readily recognised by at least all American readers. In the year 18—, *ante bellum*, a certain lieutenant in the army, who had graduated at the wrong end of his class at West Point, being stationed in the city of New York, was giving his friends a good deal of anxiety and trouble by his habits of intemperance. That same man, to-day, occupies the highest pinnacle of political power, and sits enthroned in the temple of Republican glory! At about the same epoch—*ante bellum*—a certain lad, sitting by the driver of one of Adams & Co.'s Express teams, was in the habit of calling every afternoon at the *Evening Mirror* office for copies of the paper to distribute " along the lines." To-day, I find that active and intelligent " Express-boy " one of the millionaires of New

York, the bosom friend and favourite host of the President of the United States! During the same period there might have been seen, for six years, at the "compositor's case" in the *Mirror* office, a most industrious young man, earning from six to twelve dollars a week, saving half of that, by type-setting. That thrifty youth, and model "typo," is now the proprietor of a newspaper that yields him an annual profit of some £50,000, and is the owner of the finest and fastest stud of horses in the world, whose stables are palaces! But there is another side to these transformation pictures. Men—and alas! women too—have fallen as well as risen in the world during these tumultuous times of war and change, of victory and defeat, of gain and loss, of glory and disgrace. But I have no heart to sketch these pictures of sadness, of misfortune, of ruin, and of death. It is enough to make one's heart weep to meet old friends, especially of the gentler and better sex, who, one short decade ago, were in the fullest enjoyment of all the blessings of health and wealth, now reduced to abject want, unable to work, ashamed to beg, and whose only hope is in death to relieve them of the insupportable burthen of existence. I will quote the words of a lady, who shall be nameless—a well-known *ante-bellum* belle of the Sunny South—addressed to an old friend at a chance meeting yesterday in Union Square. "You do not recognise me? I am the sad remains of Madame S——, of Alabama. My Northern husband spent all my fortune; then committed a crime, for which he was sentenced to five years *travaux forcés* in France. I am penniless. My poor old mother is confined to her bed. I obtained a situation among the dancers at Niblo's, at one dollar a week, to get a little bread. The theatre is now closed, and that last resource is lost." And this poor lady, when I last saw her, thirteen years ago, was radiant in beauty and sparkling with jewels! I know well the history of the brute this unhappy woman called her husband. I shall never forget one outrageous letter he had the impudence to address to General John C. Breckinridge, in London, abusing the Ex-Vice-President of the United States for "treason." The writer of that insolent and self-complacent letter assumed infinite credit for being "truly loyal," while at the same time he was "splurging" all over Europe on the proceeds of the very robberies for which he is now undergoing his five years' term of penal servitude in France. Our sense of justice is satisfied in the punishment inflicted upon the rascal husband, while the sentiment of pity weeps over the still harder punishment endured by the innocent wife. In the sententious and often iterated refrain of Horace, "such is life." Dropping the curtain on these living *chiaro-'scuros*, a minor chord of memory being touched, let us for a moment descend into "the Valley of the Shadow of Death." Here the transformation scene may well "give us pause." It literally takes away one's breath. "Every old friend I meet is either dead or busted," was the Hibernian remark that escaped my lips in reply to the question, "How do you find New York?" At a certain farewell dinner, given at the New York Hotel on the eve of my departure for Europe in 1861, out of the twenty-four guests at the table nine are in their graves. The pleasant and familiar faces of Judge Whiting, Judge Robertson, John Van Buren, Henry J. Raymond, Charley May, Horace Clarke, Isaac Fowler, James T. Brady, I meet no more at the clubs, in the streets, or at the convivial board; while scores of others of less note, and fewer years, are sleeping in "Greenwood" or in "Woodlawn" the sleep that knows no waking. And yet in both of these sweet cities of the dead I hear the same joyous music of the birds, and inhale the same delicious aroma of the flowers.

Man dies, but Nature lives; and we recall the sad lament of Mrs Hemans—

"Woe that the Linden and the Vine should bloom,
And a just man be gathered to the tomb."

Of all my senior contemporaries, the venerable poet Bryant, the "Last Minstrel," alone remains at his *post*. Thurlow Weed and Watson Webb "still live," but off duty, on full pay. Noah, Hale, Halleck, Croswell, Ritchie, Gales, King, Bennett, Greeley, Brooks—all are at rest.

"Green be the turf above them,
Friends of my better days!"

And Fitzgreene Halleck, too, author of the above lines, and of the immortal "Marco Bozzaris"—he, too, is gone; and Louis Gaylord Clarke, with his inseparable and "boon" companion, Charley Elliott, the greatest portrait-painter of modern times. And Morris and Willis, old friends and editorial partners, a brace of brilliant poets, who enjoyed life so thoroughly that one could not help wishing they might live for ever, were in the very heyday flush of existence—their visiting cards, also, are tombstones now. But this will not do. I am getting blue. The "dead sleep well." They need neither sympathy nor tears, and regrets are unavailing. As for old friends "busted," God help them, in a city where the "almighty dollar" is of more consequence to personal consideration than in any other city in the world. A "dead beat" is a nuisance anywhere, but in money-worshipping New York he is worse off than a "stump-tail bull in fly-time," to use the forcible dialect of the country. I have just met a well-known citizen, whose charitable donations exceed 300,000 dollars during the last fifteen years, upon whose character there has never been a spot, blemish, or wrinkle, who, under a momentary eclipse of fortune, declares he "does not know where he could borrow one hundred dollars." Truly "Fortune is blind" as well as fickle, and much given to making "misdeals." There sat behind me at the Hippodrome last night an exceedingly vulgar-looking woman, whose coarse, unamiable, and ungrammatical talk with her little boy, whom she called "Jim Fiske," attracted my attention, and her fingers were covered with diamonds that a Duchess might envy! One word touching Rochefort's meteoric *fiasco*. A compound rabble of French refugees, including Communists, Red Republicans, Internationalists, *et id hoc genus*, attempted, by exhibiting the infamous editor of the scurrilous *Lanterne* as a "lion," to raise money, ostensibly for the "poor ill-treated convicts of New Caledonia." A long rigmarole of abuse of all the better classes in France, got up by Rochefort, appeared in the *Herald*, by way of advertising the performance at the Academy of Music. There were not five hundred persons in the house, including "deadheads," and Rochefort was so chagrined at his lack of attraction to the New York public, that he left at an early hour the next morning for England, under the false pretence of having received a "pressing telegram from his daughter." Arrangements to lecture in Philadelphia and Boston, where halls had been engaged, and posters issued, were countermanded. Instead of raising "aid and comfort" for his fellow-convicts, the net proceeds of the "show" at the Academy was not enough to pay the "Lion's" hotel bill. America has no sympathy with French iconoclasts, and, least of all, with the bloodthirsty incendiaries of the Commune. Rochefort has disgusted the entire press of New York by his lying statement that "the war of 1870 was a war of personal aggrandisement, and that Napoleon III. knowingly determined to sacrifice the lives of 200,000 men in order to secure the privilege of banishing 500!" This malignant and conceited agitator will, no doubt, attempt to organise mischief, either in England or in Switzerland. If there is no extradition law to reach such wholesale criminals as he, there ought to be one passed without delay. In regard to the political situation in France, untravelled Americans are hopeful for the Republic; while the better-informed class, who know something of the French people from personal observation, are predicting and praying for the restoration of the Empire. The candidate is ready, and the people are more than willing. The grandson of Hortense, the great-grandson of Josephine, has a lineage and a legend dear to the heart of France.

THE PARK.

THE New Yorkers may well boast of their Central Park. Its beauties are simply superlative, and cannot be exaggerated. The natural advantages of these superb pleasure-grounds—embracing some eight hundred acres—are unequalled in any city of Europe, while good taste in embellishment brings the Park within the domain of the Fine Arts. Excellent roads, flourishing trees, sparkling fountains, placid lakes, a profusion of flowers, with here and there a statue to some cosmopolitan demigod, make up a panorama equally pleasant to look upon and to reflect upon. I know not what this great luxury has cost the taxpayers of New York; but its benefits to the people cannot be estimated in dollars and cents, and the blessings of posterity will flow, like an ever-deepening river, upon the memory of its originators. As Sancho Panza "blessed the man who invented sleep," I cannot refrain from a passing benediction on the sweet air which I breathed there yesterday, redolent of new-mown hay and the balm of a thousand flowers. With few exceptions, the equipages one sees in the Park have a fast, ambitious, pretentious appearance, altogether unlike the quiet dignity of Hyde Park and other Old World drives. Everybody is trying to pass everybody, and both carriages and horses seem to be made for show and speed, rather than for comfort and endurance. The public caution against driving in the Park at a rate of over seven miles an hour, like too many other laws and ordinances in this country, is evidently a "dead letter." Two ideas seem to have taken possession of the American mind during the past decade—size and speed; vastness and rapidity. For universal exponents of these ideas, observe the horses, the houses, the women, and the churches. The latter present a most striking feature in these transformation scenes. All the little old down-town churches, built in the latter half of the last century and the first half of the present, have been transplanted to the upper part of the city, mostly in the Fifth Avenue, where they now stand in grand expansion and in full bloom. Notwithstanding the high price of lots in this fashionable locality, to use the popular phrase, congregations of all denominations have stuck at no cost to secure a site for their temples to —— in the street of palaces, which seems to be regarded as the only avenue to Paradise—and "good society." Here the Roman Catholics are building a marvellously fine marble Cathedral, which has more the air of an "effete Old World institution" than anything we have ever seen in America. And here, too, we find the old "Dutch Reformed Church," disguised in such a magnificent pile of "frozen music" as to suggest the propriety of changing its name to the "Dutch *Transformed* Church." On almost every block from Murray Hill to Central Park there towers a lofty, ornate "House of God," some of whose spires reach as far towards heaven as the law of gravitation will permit. "The children cry for bread, and ye give them stones," in the shape of sumptuous churches. We are complacently told that not less than 700,000,000 of dollars are invested in the various institutions and denominations of Religion in the United States. And yet the Almshouses are full, and Prisons too—crime being the natural offspring of poverty. Certain brave heretics, of "advanced ideas," are beginning to have the courage to ask if it would not be wise to devote a little more attention to the wants of man, and a little less pomp and circumstance to the "glory of God," who needs nothing from human hands, not even the poor lip-service and pious "praises" of miserable sinners! Instead

of more ostentatious churches, more costly temples
dedicated to "Him who dwelleth not in temples
made with hands," the common welfare of man
demands a multiplication of soup-houses, bath-
houses, and school-houses. To catch the little
street Arab, wash him, feed him, and educate him,
is the first duty of every community to its pauper
children. The "wicked" proprietor of the New
York *Herald*, who gave 30,000 dollars last winter
to feed the starving poor of New York, did more
real good than all the prayers of all the churches.
It is high time that the mythologies and traditions
of musty "Religions," based on ignorance and
superstition, should be exploded. The most cultivated intellect of the world is logical, rational,
and has faith only in the religion of practical
charity, the tangible religion of the soup-house,
instead of the empty ceremonies of the church.
But I am venturing on a transformation scene of
the future, and perhaps a little too remote a future,
even for my most cosmopolitan reader. The time
will come, however, when these "temples of God"
will be pointed to as the follies of man, and when
temples to humanity shall be everywhere erected
instead. In those "better days" for the coming
race, disease and deformity will not be allowed to
multiply, and "replenish the earth" with criminals;
but there will be at least as much attention paid

to improving the breed of man as the breed of horses and the "lower animals." The world moves—the moral as well as the physical world. Only last Sunday the Rev. Henry Ward Beecher rose to the courage of his convictions, and declared his disbelief in the Book of Genesis, including the Garden of Eden fable, and the Mosaic account of the Creation. To come down to minor observations. Tobacco-chewing and squirting among gentlemen is subsiding. The sidewalks and marble steps are no longer covered with disgusting splashes of the yellow fluid, and the everlasting spittoon is seldom inundated. European intercourse, doubtless, has something to do with this reformation. I have been somewhat surprised to see so many double-breasted women in New York; and that, too, with very *petite* figures. But on reflection—not investigation—I am reminded that this is "the land of cotton." The ladies persist in the dirty and extravagant habit of trailing the skirts of their rich silk dresses on the filthy sidewalks. Why indulge in this objectionable and uncomfortable fashion? Celebrated for their small feet, and always *bien chaussée*, it surely cannot be modesty that prevents their showing them! *La belle Américaine* has not yet learned the Parisienne's bewitching *coquetterie du pied.* Rachel used to say she could talk with her feet. Another feminine caprice puzzles me. With the mercury among the upper tens, even in the nineties, nine out of every ten ladies I meet are dressed in heavy black silk, which gives them anything but an ice-creamy appearance. In the good old *ante-bellum* days, if "Belle Brittan's" jottings can be relied on, Fifth Avenue dames and demoiselles used to promenade in light, diaphanous robes, looking as cool, as graceful, and as willing to be wooed as zephyrs. But times have changed, and fashions too; and men and women most of all. The Turkish Bath has become a "great institution" in New York, of which, and my experience therein, I shall have something to say in my next.

HEALTH.

The subject in which all of us are most deeply interested is summed up in the word *health*, which happens to rhyme with the kindred word *wealth*, representing the next " good thing " which all the world is struggling to possess. Probably the two greatest evils of life, always taking a material view of things, are sickness and poverty, the antitheses of the two supreme blessings. And when poor human nature is compelled to make the pilgrimage of life between these dismal, ill-matched companions of suffering and penury, existence is but a perpetual penance, and the grave a longed-for bed of rest. Of the two "popular evils," sickness is worse than poverty. Many a man of envied fortune—even the miser who worships gold—would gladly exchange all he possesses in houses, lands, and "securities," for the robust health, savage appetite, good digestion, and dreamless sleep of his poorest servant. Yes, not wealth, but health, is the *summum bonum* of human existence. The athlete of the Hippodrome is a happier man than the octogenarian of Wall Street, whose income is "calculated" at *eight millions of dollars a year.* Would not the veteran "Commodore," whose lifelong fight for gold is nearly finished, give, not only all his income, but his "principal" with it, to be set back in years and health to the condition in which I first knew him, thirty-five years ago, as the captain of a small river steamboat? And would any young Hercules of the Hippodrome exchange his moderate "living" for Vanderbilt's hundred millions and eighty years? There is nothing the world can give in compensation for health and youth. These are Nature's most precious gifts, but only appreciated when irrevocably lost.

> "Like birds whose beauties languish half-concealed,
> When mounted on the wing, resplendent shine in azure, green, and gold,
> So blessings brighten as they take their flight."

My good old friend, John Carter Brown, of Providence, died yesterday, leaving forty millions of dollars. All the wealth of Brown and Ives could not purchase him a substitute when drafted by that universal recruiting-officer who knocks at every door. No man can preserve his youth, nor escape the marks of "Time's effacing fingers."

We cannot, as dear Charles Lamb lamented,

"lay our ineffectual fingers upon the spokes of the great wheel," and stop where we are. Growing old is a part of the inevitable programme of life. It belongs to the natural process of gradation by which Nature accomplishes all her work, never doing anything abruptly. Men grow, and bud, and blossom, and bear fruit, or live barren, like the trees, and then, also like the trees, fade, and fall, and disappear. We have only to accept the situation; or, as Margaret Fuller said to Carlyle, "accept the universe." But while youth, the beauty of efflorescence, cannot be long retained—the flowers of spring must give place to the fruits of autumn—health is a perennial plant that may be conserved even to a "green old age." And yet, how rarely do we see men, advanced in life, like the veterans of the forest, in a state of healthy decay, to use a paradox, dying gracefully, leaf by leaf! The world is full of doctors, and the cities reek with drug-shops. Hence the universal sickness, the innumerable "complaints," with which the distressed atmosphere is thickened and infected. Man was not made to be sick, nor to spend his life in groaning and mourning. What *was* he made for then, to repeat the everlasting conundrum of the ages? I suppose man was made, like all other organised beings, both animal and vegetable, for the simple gratification of the Creative Power. Here I will hold up, and come to the practical question of health, which greatly concerns us all, especially those who have abused it, neglected it, lost it, and are now running all over the world seeking to regain it. No one's testimony in the witness-box is of any value unless he speaks of what he actually knows from experience and observation. Therefore, in what I have to say on the subject of health I must be personal. I left London one month ago, feeling miserably ill, after nine years of "hard labour and close confinement" on the treadmill of a weekly newspaper. For nearly three years I had not even inhaled a breath of country or sea-air. The result of all this over-work and incessant care was, naturally enough, torpidity of the liver, loss of appetite, a dull pain in the head, feverish dreams, depression of spirits, and a sort of *disagreeable all-overness*. (Many a reader knows how it is himself.) The only alternative was to break away, or break down. My good friends insisted on the former as the wiser conclusion, consoling me with the assurance that change of scene and comparative rest would soon repair the "editorial machine," and enable it to "work all the better for indefinite years to come." The rest on board ship, and the pure, invigorating ozone of the sea, proved a most beneficent medicine. But something more was wanting, something radical and revolutionary, and this I have found in the Turkish Bath. Scarcely had I arrived in New York, when that marvellous specimen of humanity, George Francis Train, called with a kind invitation from Dr Miller, of West Twenty-sixth Street, to come and try his "water cure," endorsed with what I may call a peremptory mandate from Mr Train himself, who claims to have the power of "pschycologising" people, and curing all who yield their "wills" to his in childlike obedience and faith. " Two Turkish Baths a day," said Train, with absolute imperiousness, "or you are a dead man within thirty days. Do as I say, and you will get well in that time. I care enough for you to cure you, and you are about the only man I care as much for. I have outgrown all limitations, all interests, all associations, all intellects. *I am above the dictatorship;* great enough to refuse it if offered me to-day. Health is the only good. Cleanliness, if next to godliness, is next *above* that sham virtue. I have taken two Turkish Baths a day for seven months, three Electric Baths a week, and have eaten no meat in all this time. I am the healthiest man in the nation, the *only* absolutely healthy man." And certainly Train's splendid physical condition, and perfect "form," as they say in England, fully endorse all his encomiums on the Bath. I tried the Miller panacea—two a day, at six o'clock A.M., and at five o'clock P.M.—for seven days, and since then one a day for two weeks, in all some thirty baths. The effect has been highly beneficial; but I attribute as much of the "improvement" to the rigid regimen as to the regular bathing. Farinaceous food, with no wine or spirits, persistently adhered to for three or four weeks, is change enough to revolutionise almost any one's "department of the interior." It requires some courage during this hot weather to enter a room at 160° Fahrenheit, and while pouring down ice-water by the quart to pour out an equal quantity of tepid water through the five millions of pores in the cuticle; yet after the "grooming," a delicious sense of coolness, cleanness, and drowsiness, more than compensates for the brief purgatory we have to pass in order to reach this Turkish paradise. Dr Miller's establishment is in great vogue in New York. People here seem to be recognising the Religion of Health as the newest and best of all the Gospels, with Miller for its priest and Train for its prophet. I will close with two questions of cosmopolitan interest: Is there any blessing equal to health? Can there be health without cleanness? As one of our own poets has said—

"Even from the body's purity
The mind receives a kindly, sympathetic aid."

TRUTH.

ASSOCIATED with Miller's Religion of Health there has recently arisen, to use an Orientalism, a new Apostle of Truth. William Henry Swartwout is the name of which the world is destined to hear much in the present age, and still more in the future. Mr Swartwout, until lately, was an active and successful business man, a manufacturer, but who, like Saul of Tarsus on the road to Damascus, has suddenly encountered a great awakening light "above the brightness of the sun," and now claims to be inspired by the infinite and eternal Soul of Truth, which compels him to speak the words of Truth and obey the voice of Truth, at all times, in all places, and on all occasions, and he is about to solve the problem whether a man can do so and live in these electro-plated days of shams, hypocrisies, and false pretences. It is a comparatively easy thing to utter the truth, and nothing but the truth; but when it comes to the whole truth—the time has not yet come for that—crucifixion of both body and soul is the penalty of the present, as well as the past, for all who dare to publish the "naked truth." Mr Swartwout is a member of Dr Adams' Presbyterian Church, one of the fashionable congregations of New York, and they have already taken steps to oust this dangerous disciple of Truth from their consecrated fold. No fault can be found with his life, his "good works," his strictly temperate habits; but the simple truths he speaks, upsetting all the old traditions and superstitions of orthodoxy, these good "Church members" cannot bear. "Christianity in its primitive purity is a good thing," says Swartwout; "let us practise it." And the simple proposition sets the Church on fire with indignation. "Away with him, away with him!" is the sentence of the pious pastor, and the whole congregation join in the chorus. But this emancipated Christian, whom the Church to-day rejects, may yet become the chief corner-stone in the Church of the future, on whose temples, dedicated to Humanity, shall be engraved, in two words, the one omnipotent creed that redeems the world and solves all enigmas—Love and Truth. In proof that he is "not disobedient unto the heavenly vision," this new Minister of the new Gospel has sold all he possessed and renounced all social considerations to follow Truth. In preparation for his great mission he does not seek the solitude of the mountain nor the sadness of the desert, but proposes to arm himself with practical knowledge by making a trip around the world, in order to obtain a comprehensive idea of the great family of man in all its present conditions and past epochs. Mr Swartwout is a thorough cosmopolitan, having outgrown the limitations and the prejudices of nationalities, races, and sects, as well as all mere social accidents, which rank men in tiers and classes one above another. To accompany him in his expedition of observation and note-taking, Mr Swartwout has selected the following "assistants:"—George Francis Train, the greatest traveller of this or any other age, as Courier; E. P. Miller, Philosopher of Health; W. E. McMaster, the well-known portrait-painter and journalist as Artist; Col. Fuller, Editor of the *Cosmopolitan*, as Historiographer. A somewhat remarkable book may be looked for as the result of this extraordinary "combination of talent." Mr Swartwout proposes to start on his spheroidal voyage about the middle of July, journeying with the sun, from New York to San Francisco, thence to Japan, China, India, Asia, Europe, arriving in England about the first of November next. The journey of 25,000 miles can be accomplished in 100 days, at the average rate of 250 miles a day, and, according to Jules Verne, the trip has been made in 80 days, or rather in 79, a day being gained by travelling against the sun. Having announced the discovery of a new risen star in the West to our readers of both hemispheres, and intimated the possibility of a new Round the World Book for the coming Christmas, I have a few more words to say of Miller's Bath Hotel, the birthplace of the New Dispensation. Mr Train imputes to the Miller system of health an entire revolution in his own feelings, character, politics, and purposes. This exuberant, eloquent, epigrammatic, and loquacious *lusus* of humanity has become, under the subduing influence of two Turkish Baths a day, thoughtful, silent, and contented. Having abstained all his life from indulgence in wine, spirits, and tobacco, "his purified system," now rejects all animal food, including even eggs and fish. And yet on a diet of farinaceous food and fruits he is all the while gaining physical strength. " Horses," says Train, " eat no meat." That the Turkish Bath does not make man physically weaker we have abundant proof in the "experts" who pass ten to twelve hours a day, most of the time in rooms at a temperature of 150° to 160° Fahrenheit. One of Miller's experts, a young Englishman, rather below the medium size, who during the last ten years has manipulated some 70,000 persons, enjoys perfect health, and can lift 700 lbs.

The female experts, who also serve as table-waiters, are the purest and healthiest-looking women I have seen in America. With all these living testimonials in favour of the Turkish Bath, I wish to withdraw a remonstrance I once made to a lady in London, who wrote me "she was taking a Turkish Bath every day," that "she would wash all the sweetness out of her." *Tout au contraire*, it is only the impurities of the system that evaporate under this sweltering temperature. The average number of bathers at Miller's is about one hundred a day, and the luxury only costs 5s., which is better than paying a guinea to the "doctor," who looks at your tongue, feels your pulse, and orders a dose of purgative poison for the benefit of his pharmaceutical friend. I believe a discount is made to the guests residing in the hotel, which embraces three first-class houses in West Twenty-sixth Street, and is one of the cheapest and best hotels in New York. The proprietor contemplates a building of great magnitude, constructed solely for health and comfort. It would not be a bad idea for A. T. Stewart to convert his unfinished "Asylum" in the Fourth Avenue into an immense Free Bath establishment. This suggestion may also be commended to Mr James Lick, who has recently executed his own Will by giving millions to the Charities of San Francisco. Mr

Stewart's magnificent marble pile is a standing mystery to the people of New York, no progress having been made towards its completion for the last two or three years. But Mr Stewart is doing a work of glorious fame at his Garden City on Long Island, which ought to be called Stewartville in honour of the founder. The houses are of three uniform classes—for men of wealth, for men of moderate incomes, and for the poor who have to work for daily bread. The streets of this ideal City are broad boulevards, lined with trees, and twenty-five years hence it will no doubt be one of the most attractive places in America. This is a sort of monument worthy of the noblest ambition. Mr Stewart, who has reached the allotted milestone of threescore and ten, is estimated to be worth from £10,000,000 to £20,000,000, and has no children. Why not, like the California millionaire, "administer" his own estate? How much "good" he might accomplish by bestowing a million or two on some brave, high-toned newspaper, devoted to the propagation of cosmopolitan ideas; and what a grand obituary he would have!

MONEY.

THE suspension of the old conservative banking-house of Turner Brothers has created equal surprise and regret in Wall Street. This eminently respectable firm, consisting of six industrious brothers, was established in 1844, and has sustained a high character for integrity, prudence, and solidity, for thirty years, having passed through many panics unshaken. After the financial tornado of last autumn it was generally believed that all the Wall Street firms left standing were " good " for many years to come, and none were regarded with more confidence than the name of Turner Brothers. That they should be compelled to stop payment when money was "a drug in the market," at 2 per cent. a year, " at call," took the street by surprise. The firm has not yet made any official statement of their affairs, but it is generally understood that " advances " to a Western Railroad Company, to the amount of some 1,500,000 dols., is the cause of their collapse—a repetition of the law of cause and effect which brought down Jay Cooke & Co., Henry Clews & Co., and Fisk & Hatch. This latter firm are now paying off their debts in anticipation of the time fixed in their "extension agreement." Although there is a great "tendency downwards" in Wall Street, yet with the approaching adjournment of Congress, when tinkering at finance laws will be suspended for a few months, a general revival of business is expected. The crops of all descriptions, and in all sections of the country, are full of promise. It is estimated that the surplus wheat crop of California this year will exceed the average wheat export of Russia. There is great agricultural prosperity also in Texas, which I have long regarded as the most attractive State in the Union for European emigration. It has no debt, and can easily supply the world with cotton, corn, and cattle. Therefore, although business is dull, I have no sympathy with the croakers who are all the time predicting financial disasters. The United States possess exceptional and unlimited resources. The people are not confined to the ordinary products of agriculture and manufactures, as in France and most other countries; but they dig no end of material wealth out of the earth in the form of precious metals. From statistics now before me, I find that the aggregate yield of the last quarter of a century reaches the stupendous sum of 1,583,644,934 dollars. Of this, California produced about three-fourths, or 1,094,919,098, nearly all of which was in gold. Nevada has produced in gold and silver, but chiefly in the latter, 221,402,412 dollars. Most of this has come from the wonderful Comstock lode. Utah, which has but recently begun to be developed, is credited with 18,527,537 dollars, Montana with 119,308,147 dollars. Idaho has contributed 57,249,117 dollars, and Colorado 30,000,000 dollars. Oregon and Washington territories have given 25,504,250 dollars, and British Columbia 9,000,000 dollars. Arizona, which is just beginning to be worked, will probably prove the richest region of all. The increased yield last year was about 14 per cent., being 80,287,436 against 70,236,914 dollars in 1872. A country with these immense resources is not likely to have much difficulty in paying the "balance of trade;" and as this balance is now turning in favour of the United States, there is a good prospect of paying off the entire National Debt within the next twenty years. The whole amount of the debt, some 2,200,000,000 of dollars, will, no doubt, be gathered from the various gold and silver mines of the West before another ten years come round. While, therefore, it is the duty of the publicist and the economist to protest against public corruption and private extravagance in money matters, there is no lack of good and substantial reasons for taking a hopeful view of the financial future of the Republic. The population and wealth of the country are rapidly increasing, and the National Debt is diminishing at the rate of 50,000,000 dollars a year. George Francis Train, who, in his present taciturn mood, represents one of the most remarkable "Transformation Scenes" I have met in America, still insists, when he deigns to speak, that evil days are coming. In a state of general disgust, with himself, and everything else, he finds rottenness and corruption everywhere. And yet he has a practical eye to the future, as the following letter, just posted to the forty-eight New York Savings Banks, will show. I am inclined to think that the American Eagle is only moulting, and that when new fledged with his Omaha feathers he will scream louder than ever :—

"*To the Savings Banks of New York and Brooklyn.*

"The two hundred millions deposited in the names of half a million working-men in the New York and Brooklyn Savings Banks I am afraid is more or less locked up. A thousand Turkish Baths have put me in savage health, by eradicating the miasma and poison of the Tombs. I am besieged by the bears and speculators to lecture at the Academy and throughout the country, at dollar tickets, on these questions:—1. Does the money on deposit really belong to the working men and women? 2. In time of panic, financial disaster, and paralysed industry, have depositors a right to draw out their own money? 3. Should they call for it on my portraying the condition of affairs on a black-board in the lecture-halls, what would be the chances of their finding the money available? 4. In case it was not forthcoming, and Grant having peremptorily shut off all relief in case of another crisis, would there be any danger from a Communistic rising of enraged depositors, of burning the city, or resorting to personal violence against those who had squandered their hard-earned wages? I have never spoken since the Tombs outrage on liberty, although I suppose I could take thirty thousand dollars the coming season in arousing the people to the coming disasters of plague, panic, repudiation, and civil war; but you will see by the enclosed that I wish to leave the country for my fourth trip round the world. Before starting, as money is quoted at 2 and 3 per cent., I wish to negotiate a mortgage on my Omaha property. I own between four and five hundred acres of city lots—say five thousand (N.Y. size)—within the city limits, on which I will give you a first mortgage, and an undisputed title, for a loan, for a term of years, for one hundred thousand dollars. The property, properly advertised, should sell, even in these days of stagnation, for several times that. As I do not wish to speak again, I write this to ask at what rate you will advance the sum stated. I shall not require any portion of it before the 1st of next January, and the balance will not be wanted before January 1st, 1876. My Wall Street bankers will show you the record of a clear title, and any Omaha capitalist will certify as to the value of the security. Will you oblige me with an early answer?

— GEO. FRANCIS TRAIN.

"MILLER'S TURKISH BATH HOTEL,
   41 W. 26th St., N.Y.
     June 18, 1874."

Apropos of his extraordinary "evolutions" in body and mind, which Train attributes to Miller's Baths and farinaceous food, the following capital letter of remonstrance from his legal adviser, Clark Bell, one of the leading lawyers of New York, contains enough of both wit and argument to entitle it to a permanent record in the columns of the *Cosmopolitan*:—

"DEAR GEORGE FRANCIS TRAIN,—I look upon your attempt to make yourself fat with no little interest, and shall watch your progress to triumphant obesity without concern or dismay. Your feet not being divided or cloven, you are not naturally a granivorous animal. Vegetables and grains soonest make fat and fill up the cellular tissue. If we wish a fat ox, we confine him wholly to vegetable food and grains; ditto of the swine. When I saw you yesterday, you had commenced growing fat. I never saw you with so much of the superfluous. Eat largely of bread and sugar, and you will grow fat sooner. Read Bantam, and he will teach you many things in this rare struggle. The lion living on meat never grows fat, and is emblematic of courage and strength. The whole feline family develop muscle, tenacity, and even ferocity, without adipose matter, hating grains, and only tasting vegetables as a medicine, or a preventative. In agriculture we place our prize animals in close quarters, give them little exercise, and only grain and vegetables to eat. They soon generate carbon, and become puffed up with fatness. In all *rôles* you have won distinction and commanded success. How it will be in this race for ponderosity I do not know; but I doubt not you will win as before. You must not, however, always be saddened by the reflection that while you may become a second Daniel Lambert, you cannot make of yourself the first fat man. There is a Fat Man's Club, to which I shall soon expect you to clamour for executive honours. I do not know how long you have been cramming, but I can see, and did see, the enormous change in you yesterday. You must be gaining in fat alone from 2½ lbs. to 5 lbs. a week. The scales are near you; try them, and record your progress. Fatness is not necessary to human greatness, for you are already great without it. It is not an accessory or aid even to genius. For a man who has become ennuied of all the successes of life, *blasé* of the world, bilious of the hour, *dégoûté* of time and denies eternity, I know no more fit refuge than the *otium cum dignitate* of laughing and growing fat. Go on, granivorous and vegetable seeker after truth, quiet, and repose. Build up the cellular, lay on the adipose, so that if cremation comes, you will make a good fire and burn with a blaze, without either kindling or kerosene.—I remain, watching, faithfully yours, CLARK BELL.

"NEW YORK, *May* 18, 1874."

The point of the joke is to be picked from the fact that Train has a horror of growing fat. According to the weighing record of the Bath Hotel, when he entered the establishment seven months ago, his weight was 217 lbs. To-day he rejoices in 203 lbs., a decrease of 14 lbs. But this falling off in "adipose matter" he attributes to other causes than abstinence from animal food. On this question Mr Bell has decidedly the best of the argument. There is no doubt that a carnivorous diet will make men lean, and that granivorous food will make them fat. Neither is there any doubt that Nature made man an omnivorous animal; and Nature is wiser than the doctors.

CONGRESS.

On Monday, June 21st, President Grant signed the Currency Bill, the most important Act of the last Session of Congress, and stocks in Wall Street instantly jumped from 2 to 5 per cent. The reason of the rise was owing, not so much to approbation of the measure, as to the general satisfaction that the volume of currency was finally "fixed," and that the question of expansion or contraction was no longer left to the caprice of the Treasury Department. The Bill is by no means in accordance with the President's famous "Memorandum" addressed to Senator Jones, which was regarded as a Veto in advance; but it gives the business public a definite basis to stand on, at least until the meeting of Congress in December. And this positive benefit is everywhere hailed with satisfaction. The "Bulls" of the Stock Exchange, for the first time in ten months, are particularly hopeful and happy. Only a few weak and obstinate "Bears," in attempting to resist the "upward tendency," have succumbed. Altogether, the change in the street during the last three or four days amounts to a veritable transformation. On the 22d June Congress adjourned, and the nation drew a long breath. This and all other countries suffer more from over-legislation than from lack of legislation. Half-a-dozen fundamental laws are quite enough for the government of men, and of empires; and if all the statute-books in existence were burned, and only the Golden Rule left, there would be more justice, if less law, in the administration of affairs, both public and private. On the whole, the people seem well contented with what Congress has done, still more so with what it has not done. There has been an aggregate diminution of 27,000,000 dollars in the general "appropriations," which may be credited to the account of national economy, a gratifying item for the taxpayer. The District of Columbia Ring has been broken up, although the debts of the District, which the nation will have to pay, are something like 30,000,000 dollars. Strange to say, under the new law, providing for three Commissioners to govern the Capital Territory of ten miles square, the President had the audacity to nominate "Boss Shepherd," the deposed Ringleader, as Chairman! No Presidential act in the whole history of the Government has ever so shocked and surprised the people as this. The Senate, composed of a large majority of the President's political friends, indignantly rejected the nomination by a vote of 36 to 6. The President's motive for thus insulting the common sense of the country is variously conjectured. Grant's personal friends attribute it to a sort of dogged devotion to a bosom crony against a perfect deluge of popular obloquy. And with this best of all possible excuses for the outrageous nomination, I will leave the matter, to be revived with telling effect when the question of a Third Term comes up. In calling Mr Hale into his Cabinet, as Postmaster-General, in place of Mr Creswell, resigned, the President has given great satisfaction to all parties; and this may be said, also, of the nomination of Mr Cattell, in place of Shepherd, rejected, which was unanimously confirmed by the Senate. Mr Cattell, late United States Senator from New Jersey, is favourably known in London as Government agent for the conversion of United States 6's into 5's. For some two months there will be a lull in politics; and yet every watering-place will be a sort of caucus for settling the preliminaries of the "fall campaign" for the election of representatives to the next Congress. It is generally predicted, even by the Republicans, that the Democrats, or Conservatives,

will have a decided majority in the Congress of
1876. If Grant is really "laying pipe" for a
Third Term, it is very evident he intends to break
with the Black Republicans, and throw himself into
the hands of a new party—a party which proposes
to win under the banner of Free Trade and Real
Money—that is, specie payment. But I have yet
to find here, as in England, the first indication of
an out-and-out Free Trade party. As I have often
published, without fear of contradiction, or, I
should rather say, with no hope of contradiction,
the *Cosmopolitan* is the only absolute, logical Free
Trade newspaper in either hemisphere. All the
so-called Free Trade journals on this side, as on
the other, advocate "strictly revenue tariffs"—
approximate Free Trade. This is all nonsense;
as well advocate approximate honesty. Any measures that stop short of the immediate abolition
of Custom-Houses are mere half-measures, and
worse than none. Let the whole thieving army of
Custom-House agents, spies, and informers be at
once disbanded, and put to some honest occupation
whereby to earn their daily bread, instead of stealing it, and the commerce of the world would get
rid of an *incubus* that makes trade a trick and a
struggle, and business a penance instead of a
pleasure. The resources, the labour, the enterprise, and the ingenuity of America need no

protection, other than the broad Atlantic, to compete successfully with any other nation on the globe. The tide of exchange is beginning to turn in favour of the United States, and the people are beginning to see and to feel, in their pockets, that the tax on foreign importations robs millions of poor consumers to enrich a few hundreds of millionaire manufacturers. Besides, it is estimated that not more than one-half of the " tolls " taken at the Custom-House ever reaches the Treasury of the United States. Therefore, abolish the whole system of fraud and corruption, and come down to the only honest and legitimate tax for the support of Government—a direct tax on property. Under this latter just, simple, economical policy, we should never see a repetition of the disgraceful scene witnessed in the House of Representatives on Friday night last, when, with the mercury bubbling among the "upper tens," the Hall was packed with thousands of men, women, and niggers to hear "Old Cock-eye Butler" defend the Custom-House spy system, and denounce the eminent firm of Phelps, Dodge, & Co., of New York, and Phelps, James, & Co., of Liverpool, for defrauding the Government—in other words, for stealing millions by swearing to false invoices. This firm has imported, mostly in metals, during the last forty years, goods amounting to 400,000,000 of dollars. Mr W. E. Dodge, the venerable head of the firm, is Chairman of the New York Chamber of Commerce, and President of the Young Men's Christian Association, a man of large wealth and high social position. General Butler accuses him of obtaining his vast wealth, and, consequently, his social position—to use plain English—by *theft* and *perjury!* And the galleries applaud him to the echo. But the press, of all parties and sections, is pouring multitudinous vials of hot indignation upon the bald head of the heartless "Beast." But why did Phelps, Dodge, & Co., if entirely innocent, pay the Government some 270,000 dollars to "compromise" a claim for millions? Because we suppose a lawsuit would have cost them a much greater sum. Jordan, Marsh, & Co., of Boston, against whom a similar charge is pending for a very large amount, are showing fight and showing pluck. As a matter of *principle*, the man who pays an unjust claim condones a fraud; but the world, especially the business world, is governed by interest, not principle. The merchant's motto is, of two evils choose the least; a woman's, of two offers accept the first. "The Plymouth Church Scandal" is again the uppermost topic of the day; and although the *Cosmopolitan* has little stomach for such garbage, to ignore the matter entirely would be unfaithful to the history of current events. Briefly, then, as possible, the scandal is this:—The Rev. Henry Ward Beecher, who for the last twenty-five years has played a star *rôle* at the Brooklyn Plymouth Church, where his religious merchandise brings him a revenue of £10,000 a year, was accused some four or five years ago, by his bosom friend and Christian Church brother, Theodore Tilton, of the greatest crime that man can possibly commit against man. I need not name it to cosmopolitan readers. At the same time Mr Tilton withdrew from the Church, whose " unco guid " pastor he could not but regard as a hypocrite, pure and simple. The scandal got wind, but, except through the columns of a certain disreputable sheet, the Press, giving the " great and good man " the benefit of its doubt, had but little to say on the subject. In the meantime there was a melting meeting between the accused and his accuser, which resulted in apparent penitence on one hand, forgiveness on the other, and everlasting silence on both. But a certain meddlesome body, called the " Church Council," composed of a synod of Presbyterian Churches, affiliated with Beecher's, under the lead of the Rev. Leonard Bacon, raked open the buried offal, for the purpose of whitewashing Beecher and blacksmearing Tilton; whereupon the latter comes out in his newspaper—the

Golden Age—with a minute history of the whole infamous affair. And the columns of all the newspapers are to-day regaling the prurient appetites of their myriads of readers with the "great sensation scandal." Beecher and his "followers," it is announced, have resolved to treat Tilton's charges with silent contempt. This is a very cheap and easy way of meeting evidence directed against the "Lord's anointed." But the blind and foolish world is slow to believe anything against its cherished idols. Pious people, who have been taught from their cradles to sing the praises of good King David, never think of the wicked passion that got rid of Gen. Uriah, in order to get possession of his beautiful wife. The Saints of the Ancient Bible, and the Saints of the Modern Church, like Kings, "can do no wrong" in the eyes of their infatuated believers. The Rev. Henry Ward Beecher, who, by talking religion two or three hours in the week, enjoys an income that enables him to keep fast horses, a mansion in town, a summer residence in the country, and to live on the fat of the land, is morally infallible in the eyes of Plymouth Church, notwithstanding his sensuous mouth and dominant cerebellum. But here is an extract from his own written confession to his outraged "brother in Christ." There is but one construction to be given to it by any one who pretends to an average share of common sense :—

"I ask Theodore Tilton's forgiveness, and humble myself before him as I do before my God. He would have been a better man in my circumstances than I have been. I can ask nothing except that he will remember all the other breasts that would ache. I will not plead for myself. I even wish that I were dead. H. W. BEECHER.

"BROOKLYN, *January* 1, 1871."

If this is not a forgery, and its genuineness has not been questioned, the great jury of the public will regard it as the abject confession of a guilty man; and that, too, of an outrage intensified a thousand times by the intimate and sacred relation of the parties; and again, ten thousand times more by the garb of hypocrisy which cloaks and seeks to conceal the sin.

DOGS.

"Every dog has his day," says the old adage. Just now in New York every day is having at least a hundred dogs sacrificed to the hydrophobia panic; and not without reason. In spite of all the scepticism on the subject of canine poison or *rabies*, three deaths have recently occurred in this city from dog-bites, which have caused universal alarm, and raised the war-cry of " Death to dogs!" without regard to race, variety, or value. Miss Ada Clare, well known as a critic, an actress, and a *bel esprit*, was slightly bitten last winter by the pet poodle of a friend, and died in a few weeks, a victim to the subtle poison. Last week a Brooklyn dog-fancier and dealer, by the name of Butler, died a terrible death from the same cause; and this week the papers are full of the details of the horrors and agonies of M'Cormick, the butcher, who also died from the bite of a pet dog, a mere scratch on the first knuckle of the forefinger of the right hand. The physical sufferings of Mr

M'Cormick, as described in the *Tribune*, are too painful for publication. The half-a-dozen doctors who stood by the bed of the poor man, writhing in agony, foaming at the mouth, biting his tongue, and doubling himself up, even in his straight-jacket, should have put an end to his intolerable torture by instant death. The case was utterly hopeless. It is said no patient has ever recovered from a well-pronounced attack of hydrophobia. It would be an act of mercy, therefore, to kill the victim and spare his mortal agonies—quite as much so as it is the humane duty of the public executioner to finish his horrible work as swiftly as possible. Strange to say, we hear less sympathy expressed for these mad-dog victims than for the " poor dogs " themselves; and this morbid phenomenon is chiefly owing to the great activity and philanthropy—if the word may be used in this connection—of the " Society for the Prevention of Cruelty to Animals," at the head of which Mr Henry Bergh has conspicuously figured for some years past. And, like all hobby-riders, Mr Bergh has ridden this tenderness to the brute creation hobby down to the very *reductio ad absurdum*. When the City Council passed an ordinance offering a bribe of fifty cents for every stray unmuzzled dog caught and brought to the "Pound," or Dog Prison, to be put to death, if not claimed and redeemed in forty-eight hours, Mr Bergh proposed that the sentence should be inflicted by means of carbonic acid gas. And so this sentimental lover of his poor dumb brothers protracts their mortal agony some thirty minutes, while less than three minutes suffices to drown a dog, or any other quadruped or biped; and the latter mode of death is conceded by all who have attempted it, and *almost* succeeded, to be rather pleasant than painful, after the first gasp of suffocation is over. The real "cruelty" of this canine *phobia* consists in the brutal hunt after the poor creatures in the streets by heartless men and boys, who bring them, half dead, in cart-loads to the "Pound" for the sake of the reward. It would be much more humane to appoint a squad of policemen to scour the streets, and catch the stray dogs with tempting food, or words of delusive kindness. In Philadelphia, where the same anti-dog mania is raging, no less than 2500 dogs were slaughtered last week on the altar of Public Safety. And this dog-war is becoming a burning question in society, causing endless "differences" in family circles. The ladies of a certain class, notoriously fond of poodles, and tolerant of "puppies," plead eloquently for the innocence of their pets, in spite of the unanswerable and alarming fact that, in each of the above fatal cases, it was the *little pet dog* that inflicted the mortal wound. Naturally enough all this excitement is developing no end of medical theories on the *rabies* question. On this, as on all other questions, "doctors differ," and that, too, so very widely, that it is safe only to draw conclusions from facts. Mere medical "opinions" do not amount to much; while the deductions of science and reason are of infinite importance. In the first place, the question is raised why dogs go mad? In Havana, a city which contains more dogs than owners, we hear little of hydrophobia; and in Constantinople, where it is considered sacrilege to kill a dog, the fear of the disease does not exist. It seems to be a well-established fact that the canine race in "a state of nature," as distinguished from the condition of dogs in "civilised society," is never afflicted with *rabies*. The reason is obvious, and need not be given. Again, the popular fallacy that mad dogs have a horror of water is exploded. On the contrary, they are fond of putting their noses into water when the fever is on them, and biting at it as they bite at everything else, animate or inanimate; so the term "hydrophobia" is altogether a misnomer, and must be dropped from the medical dictionary. That the victims of the bite imitate in their mortal agonies the barking of dogs is explained by the spasmodic effort to eject the foam and saliva constantly flowing from the mouth, as in the case of the stalwart butcher, M'Cormick. It is simply a choking sound, resembling the short, muffled bark of a dog asleep. Having devoted sufficient space to the subject of dog-madness to induce a little precautionary reflection, the reader will doubtless appreciate the following :—

DIRECTIONS FOR THE PREVENTION OF HYDROPHOBIA.—1. A dog that is sick from any cause should be watched and treated carefully until his recovery. 2. A dog that is sick and restless is an object of suspicion. This is the earliest peculiar symptom of hydrophobia. 3. A dog that is sick and restless, and has a depressed appetite, gnawing and swallowing bits of cloth, wood, coal, brick, mortar, or his own dung, is a dangerous animal. He should be at once chained up, and kept in confinement until his condition be clearly ascertained. 4. If, in addition to any or all of the foregoing symptoms, the dog has delusion of the senses, appearing to see or hear imaginary sights or sounds, trying to pass through a closed door, catching at flies in the air when there are none, or searching for something which does not exist, there is a great probability that he is, or is becoming, hydrophobic. He should be secured and confined without delay. 5. In case any one is bitten by a dog whose condition is suspicious, the most effective and beneficial treatment is to cauterise the wound at once with a stick of silver nitrate, commonly called "lunar caustic." The stick of caustic should be sharpened to a pencil-point, introduced quite to the bottom of the wound, and held in contact with every part of the wounded surface until it is thoroughly cauterised and insensible. This destroys the virus by which the disease would be communicated.

These "Directions" are to be publicly posted throughout the city. In case there should be no lunar caustic at hand, sucking the wound, and burning it with a hot iron is recommended, at the same time binding the limb tightly, above and below the bite, to prevent the poison from circulating in the blood. It is also recommended, that when a dog bites a person, the life of the animal should be spared, in order to know whether he is mad or not. No less than seven dogs, *suspected* of madness, were killed in New York yesterday, and thirty during the last month. In regard to the suggestion I have made in connection with this subject, that the victim of the poison should be instantly relieved by death at the hands of his medical attendant, I am aware that it will shock the moral sense even of cosmopolitan readers. It shocks my own to make it. And yet, where recovery is utterly hopeless, to inflict instant death becomes a most humane and sacred duty. *Apropos* of "shocking" suggestions, what shall we say of the pamphlet recently published in England in vindication of suicide? The title of the *brochure* is "Euthanasia," the name of the author S. D. Williams, jun., and the endorser, who has given it vogue, is Mrs Crawshay, wife of the Iron millionaire of Wales. The *Saturday Review*, the *Spectator*, and the

Fortnightly "notice" this startling production. The penal law against suicide we have always regarded as a most asinine act of legislation—a disgrace to the statutes of civilised nations. In the first place, the man who commits the "crime" of self-murder is beyond the reach of human punishment. In cases of unsuccessful attempt, the poor "felon" has already suffered enough without undergoing the penalties of the prison or the treadmill. So far as human laws are concerned, the right of self-destruction is absolute. In nine cases out of ten, self-inflicted death is no loss, neither to the suicide nor to society. It is occurring here in New York daily—pistols, Paris green, leaping from high windows, hanging and drowning being the popular modes of self-extinction. The causes are :—Rum, Religion, Poverty, and Love—that is, too much Rum, too much Poverty, not enough Religion, and not enough Love. As a general rule, the friends and relations of these "rashly importunate" death-seekers are great gainers by the loss of such encumbrances. There is no danger that the defence of suicide will ever make the cause popular or fashionable. Love of life is almost as strong as the law of gravitation or self-interest, and "everything that hath breath" will cling to life and light even when every breath is a sigh, and every sunbeam a tear. It is only the guilty coward who shirks the battle of life by voluntary death. The Rev. Henry Ward Beecher, rolling in wealth, and revelling in the luxury of fame, writes to his injured brother Tilton in a paroxysm of remorse, "I even wish I were dead." It is recorded of a romantic case of suicide in one of Goethe's celebrated fictions, that it caused an extraordinary popping of solitary pistols in the Black Forest. We do not think such is likely to be the effect of this new *Euthanasian* creed in favour of suicide. But if any "poor devils" are at all that way inclined, in order to punish some false friend or faithless lover, on the "you'll-miss-me-when-I-am-gone" threat, we advise them to do it and be done with it. The sun will continue to rise and set as before, while the universal epitaph for the tombstone of all self-destructives is—"Good riddance."

THE BRANCH.

LONG BRANCH is called the seaside capital of the United States. This is owing to the fact that President Grant has chosen the place for his summer residence, and established here a sort of country Court. In this the President has shown good sense and good taste. As a watering-place, "The Branch," as it is popularly called, possesses unrivalled attractions. In the first place, Nature has endowed it with all the essential elements of a city of pleasure. The coast, to the extent of some six miles, could not have been more perfectly adapted to watering-place wants and comforts had it been planned by a civil engineer familiar with all the modern improvements for the promotion of human happiness in the hours of leisure and relaxation. It is the only point on all the coast, from Maine to Florida, where the soft sandy shore rises abruptly to a level plateau, with beautiful house lots, all prepared for building, on the very brink of the sea, with dry foundations, and perfectly safe from the "breaking waves" of the broad Atlantic, with all their mighty momentum of three thousand miles—

"Wide rolling, foaming high, and tumbling to the shore."

The background is rich and highly cultivated, the roads level, in good condition, and the atmosphere a delicious mixture of the ozone of the sea and the odour of new-mown hay. With these outdoor fascinations, no wonder driving is the great amusement of the place; and President Grant, with his fast trotters, leads the fashion. Having passed the "glorious Fourth" at "The Branch"—a day once synonymous with noisy crowds—I was particularly struck with the sobriety and decorum of the town; and that, too, under the additional excitement of the Monmouth Park Races, which drew together all the leading sportsmen of the Union. I saw no drunkenness, heard no shouting or "patriotic" singing, and only one solitary and faint fire-cracker. Another transformation from former years, which made me feel all "abroad:" that is, anywhere but in "the land of the free and the home of the brave," on this 98th Anniversary of the Declaration of American Independence, a day that used to be celebrated with the most vociferous demonstrations of patriotic joy, with guns and drums, with bells and banners, with glowing orations and deep potations, with exultations, conflagrations, hallucinations, pistols, and fire-crackers. Of course the Stars and Stripes could be seen "by the dawn's rosy light" floating from every mast and spire; but not one strain, even from a hurdy-gurdy, of the "Star-Spangled Banner," the "Marseillaise" of America, beat the heavenward flame of devotion in the air. But, in gazing at the blue sea, and the great blue Bohemian bowl above it, I recalled the lofty, mystic words in which Emerson salutes the "Natal Day" of American Liberty—

> "Oh, tenderly the haughty Day
> Fills his blue urn with fire,
> One morn is in the mighty heaven,
> And one in our desire."

What that "one" thing is which represents the universal "desire" of this, or any other people, perhaps the sage of Concord, and perhaps future Rector of Glasgow, can explain. The "one desire" at Long Branch seemed to be to get a good seat in the grand stand, or bet on the right horse at the Races. On arriving at the West End Hotel the evening before, where long queues of anxious "arrivals" were waiting for rooms, a pleasant voice, which I recognised as one of the proprietors, said, "Keep quiet, Colonel, you will be taken care of." And so I was abundantly cared for, and Grant himself could not have been made more comfortable. That same hospitable voice first welcomed me to the St Charles in New Orleans, many and many a year ago, and introduced me to the Pompanoo. Did Jules Vernes ever have the good luck to fall in with this delicious fish in his twenty thousand leagues under the sea? If not, let him take another trip for the express purpose of making a most agreeable acquaintance. Reassured that I would be "taken care of," also, for the Races, I sat quietly looking at the departing crowd until half-past one, when a handsome carriage and pair drove up with a friend from the New Dominion, to take me out. The drive to the Course, about three miles, is very pleasant. The old familiar fields of Indian corn, golden wheat, and orchards bending with apples, pears, and peaches, gladdened both eye and heart. The words of a long-forgotten old song, like water bursting from a choked-up fountain, came gushing unaware—

> "Our Mother, the Earth, a good Mother is she,
> And to toil is to welcome her care;
> Some bounty she hangs us on every tree,
> And blesses us in the free air."

The Races, four in number, were well conducted and well contested, giving great satisfaction to an immense crowd, especially to the winners. Only in the steeplechase, resulting in the death of two valuable mares, and the serious injury of one of the riders, was there anything to mar the sport of the opening day at Monmouth Park. Fortunately these accidents occurred at the end of the last "event" on the programme. The crowd within the enclosure was as quiet and orderly as those proverbially well-behaved crowds at the races in the Bois du Boulogne. This, considering the presence of more or less of Fourth-of-Julyism, struck me as remarkable. But I have noticed a generally subdued feeling among the people here, of all classes. They are less noisy, less boastful, and less exuberant than formerly. Whether the presence of the comet, or the recent panic, has thrown them into what pious people call "a concern of mind," I do not know. The fact is apparent, whatever may be the cause. Last evening, at a grand display of fireworks in Union Square, postponed from the 4th, on account of the rain, among a dense crowd of fifty thousand people there was no noise, not even in the way of applause. It is hardly necessary to say that the West-End Hotel at Long Branch, under the management of Messrs Presbury and Hildreth, is admirably kept. The *table d'hôte* is perfectly bewildering in the bountiful superfluity and variety of its dishes. Seventy-four items on the dinner bill-of-fare, and sixty-three in the breakfast bill, are enough to make one's head swim. The system is a most pernicious and dyspeptic one, but about as difficult to get rid of as universal suffrage or a vicious currency. Dainty eaters, who have some respect for the chemical condition of their stomachs, and select their simple food with sole reference to health, have to pay for gormandisers who "pack their cylinders" with everything on the programme, alike regardless of quantity, quality, or the laws of chemical affinity. As a general rule, men do not learn to live until the last decade of life, and then only when exhausted nature lacks the force to resist abuses. One word more of this delightful place before leaving it, probably for ever. It is already a city of villas, with I do not know how many summer inhabitants. But the place is destined to grow in favour and in fame. We hear it sometimes called the Brighton of America. There is not the slightest resemblance between the two towns. Brighton is an old, compactly-built city—a pocket edition of London. In Long Branch no house touches its neighbour. Like Washington, it is a "city of magnificent distances," and of possibilities also. Real estate is rising rapidly in value, and unimproved acres are doubling in market prices every five years. The West-End Hotel property, jointly owned by Messrs Presbury and Hildreth, which embraces sixty acres, and originally cost, with all the fine buildings erected for hotel purposes, half a million of dollars, will doubtless be worth double this amount in 1880. John Hoey's splendid estate of three hundred acres, with the finest pleasure-grounds in the United States, notwithstanding the enormous sum spent on it, rises in annual value, equal to its annual cost. Twenty years hence, with a wealthy population of 100,000, the present real-estate owners of Long Branch, if they hold on to their property and to life, will all be millionaires. The great and growing cities of New York, Philadelphia, Baltimore, and Washington, will always make this their favourite summer resort; while President Grant, with an indefinite number of "terms" before him, will continue to attract thousands of courtiers, politicians, and office-seekers, who, in the absence of mosquitoes, we must regard as the only bores of the place. The President's cottage is all that can be desired in the way of a summer residence, and the same may be said of G. W. Childs's, Grant's "next friend" and nearest neighbour. In the immediate vicinity of these charming villas Mr George Pullman, of Palace-car fame and fortune, is proposing to build something that will "beat Grant." The "Branch" has an institution of civilisation which many a visitor has cause to remember—a few with satisfaction, many more with regret. Chamberlain's Club House is one of the most beautiful "gambling Hells" in America. It is sumptuously furnished, and the visitors are treated to everything they can wish to eat, drink, or smoke, and for which they generally pay dearly. In looking at the game of roulette the other evening, I saw lots of money lost, and very little won, except by "the Bank," which the proprietor frankly stated had 9 per cent. in its favour, at the same time bluntly adding," If a man plays long enough, he is sure to lose all his money." But even this prediction did not seem to cool the ardour of the players, "Greenbacks" of high denominations being staked and lost by the handful. *Apropos* of gambling, I have a story to tell by way of caution to the public, but have not space for it to-day. I will only say, beware of sharpers who accost you in Broadway as old acquaintances, and invite you to step around the corner and see them get the cash for a prize just drawn in the Havana lottery.

THE COSMOPOLITAN.

HAVING "located," to use the local word, the American office of the *Cosmopolitan* at 21 Park Row, New York, I propose, what the Imperialists of France are so anxious to make, a brief "appeal to the people." In this case, perhaps explanation would be the more appropriate word, especially as the ultra-Free Tradeism of the *Cosmopolitan* is persistently misrepresented by the Protectionists. "Your paper is altogether devoted to British interests," said an anti-Free Trade journalist last evening. Without going into the old argument, I will only repeat that practical Free Trade is not for the exclusive "interests" of any one country, but for the greatest possible good of all. With this conviction the *Cosmopolitan* looks to the Free Trade party, if such a party exists, for an increasing subscription list on this side of the Atlantic. In doubting the reality of an American Free Trade party—that is, as a political organisation—we have only to recall the action of Democratic Free Traders in Pennsylvania, Massachusetts, Louisiana, or any other State where local interests override principles, and whose representatives in Congress vote for high tariffs for the special benefit of their constituents. Outside of mere politics, I find no lack of intelligent business men, engaged in all the various industries, agricultural and mechanical, who are ready to adopt the proud and honest motto—Free Trade and Specie Payment—a fair field and no favour. To ask for protection, like a child that cannot walk alone, is a most humiliating confession of weakness. It is true that the great workshops of England and France, with their cheap labour, can underbid the American manufacturers in certain products. But what nation on the earth can compete with the United States in the great and fundamental necessities of cotton, corn, sugar, gold, silver, &c., &c. ? In wine, spirits, and coffee, America will also soon become an exporting country. D. M. Hildreth, President of the "Gold Seal Wine Company," informs me that they bottled 150,000 dozen of champagne last year, which is in great demand here at two dollars a bottle, and that he has just had an order for ten cases from London. This is but one straw on the current of trade that shows which way the tide is flowing. Another item : Mr Appleton, of the American Watch

Company, tells me that they have recently opened a house in Hatton Garden, London, for the purpose of supplying the United Kingdom with perfect time-keepers, much cheaper than they can be made by any of the old manufacturers, either in Liverpool, Geneva, or anywhere else in Europe. These watches are made mostly by machinery, and are so absolutely accurate as almost to justify the boast of "regulating the sun." Having been governed in our own personal "movements" by one of these Waltham chronometers for the last fifteen years, our confidence in its veracity is infinitely greater than our faith in the infallibility of the Pope, or any other man—or woman. Mr Appleton, of course, is an advocate for free trade in watches; but there is no import tax imposed by the Government of England on watches, and the American Watch will soon be "all the go" in London. The building, at the corner of Broadway and Bond Street, in which the gold cases for these watches are made by the hundred thousand, is one of the largest and handsomest in New York. The topmost story, filled with machinery, and "operatives" of both sexes, is as neat and clean as a drawing-room. Skilled workmen, imported from the dingy and dirty workshops of England and Switzerland, open their eyes, and mouths too, at these transformation scenes. The "movements" or "works" are manufactured in Waltham, Massachusetts, where some 500 operatives are employed. One more illustration of the progress of Free Trade, not as a party principle, but as the result of practical experience. A. T. Stewart, the greatest merchant and the greatest importer in the world, is a strong advocate of absolute Free Trade. On this question Mr Stewart's individual opinion is worth more than all the crude theories of professional politicians, and all the fallacies of protection philosophers of the *Tribune* School. It may be said that Mr Stewart's *interest* lies in the direction of Free Trade, and that the hundreds of millions he has paid into the Federal Treasury as "duties" during the last forty years weigh heavily in his argument. Admit it to be so. All men reason from their pockets. But these untold millions do not represent the importer's *losses*, only the mountain of taxes levied on consumers. Free Trade would greatly increase the business of the importer and the transporter of foreign goods, while lowering the selling price to the full amount of the tariff. This, with the immediate abolition of all Custom-Houses, and the instant dismissal of the great army of Custom-House thieves and "suckers," is the first plank in the *Cosmopolitan's* platform. And on this account, chiefly, we feel justified in appealing to the genuine, honest Free Traders of America to give us their support in this great cause, the true Gospel of Commerce, by sending their names—and cheques—to our American Bureau, 21 Park Row, New York. For nine years we have been pulling at this uphill load in London, endeavouring to solve the problem whether it is possible to establish a paying newspaper in any city of the world, independent of sect, party, clique, or nationality. We have outlived a good deal of latent prejudice, and not a little active opposition, both open and covert. The question of success is now reduced to one of health, and in that regard we have cause to be hopeful. With the fall of the Empire the *Cosmopolitan* lost its best friend and most powerful support. The Emperor of the French cordially endorsed every plank in our platform; and "what can I do to assist you?" were the generous and encouraging words with which His Majesty received our earliest issue. "The gods help those who strive to help themselves;" and Hercules at last gives a lift to the poor man who has struggled hard to raise his load. "But why do you publish it in London?" I am asked. "The *Cosmopolitan*, with its liberal, world-wide views of things, might just as well, in this age of electric affinities, be issued in any other city." This would be quite true, were it not that London is such an admirable and economical workshop. Printing, paper, rent, and clerks, cost fifty per cent. more in New York. Besides, London is the *largest* city in the civilised world, and contains the best and the worst of everything, not even excepting the climate. Therefore, the " Great Metropolis " is the fittest locality for a cosmopolitan newspaper; and we believe our American readers, as a general rule, prefer their weekly *résumé* of Old World affairs, as they do their current literature and fashions, "fresh from abroad." Henceforth, news from Europe for Americans, and news from America for Europeans, will be the ruling motive in the " make-up " of the *Cosmopolitan*. With a regular correspondent in the capital of American commerce, literature, fashion, and finance, who has had large experience in journalism, associated with an active business agent, we may reasonably hope for a largely-increased circulation in the United States, the New Dominion, the West Indies, Mexico, and throughout the "whole boundless Continent." We also propose to establish agencies in all the large cities of the United Kingdom and on the Continent. With the broadest and best name for a newspaper to be found in any lexicon or language, the *Cosmopolitan* is ambitious to embrace the entire globe. [No allusion to our Conservative pink-faced contemporary next door.] While on the interesting subject of "ourselves," I deem it nothing more than justice to the "truth of history" to call attention to the statement repeatedly made by the London correspondent of the New York *Tribune*, that a certain weekly in London, not yet three months old, "is the *only* newspaper in Europe owned and edited by an American." The writer of this paltry falsehood *knows* that he is publishing an untruth. If being born near Plymouth Rock, a lineal descendant of Thomas Fuller, "the Shakespeare of the pulpit," and living forty years in America, does not make a man a "native," pray what does? But I attach not the slightest importance to the accident of parentage or birthplace. None of us are permitted to *select* either. Only these spiteful and persistent falsehoods, like certain offensive insects, may as well be stamped out of existence. The slightest bite sometimes conveys the deadliest venom. The friends of Mr Moran, among whom I claim to be one of the oldest and warmest, are far from being satisfied at his removal as First Secretary of the Legation in London, and appointed to a third clerkship in the State Department at Washington. Mr Moran has filled the important post at London, often acting as *Chargé d'Affaires* in the absence of Ministers, for some twenty years, and he should long since have been raised to a full mission. He is the best-educated American diplomatist in Europe, and his "promotion downwards" is —well, I will only say, Fish-y. Mr Moran's acceptance has not yet been announced, and we hope it will not be, unless the salary is very heavy and the work very light. In the meantime the newspapers, on both sides of the Atlantic, are "breaking his fall" with the softest words and the sweetest compliments. Since writing this sentence, I learn from an M. C. that the salary of the Third Assistant Secretary of State is only £900 a year. Another victim of the Fish torpedo is now sitting at my side. Mr C. H. Branscombe, for many years American Consul at Manchester, has just been recalled, and no reason assigned. At a farewell banquet given him by the leading merchants and citizens, Mr Branscombe was smothered with commendations of his personal and official character, filling columns in the Manchester papers. The ex-Consul goes to Long Branch to-night to ask the President "what it means?" *Apropos* of President Grant, whom I saw for the first time last Sunday, sitting on the piazza of his pleasant seaside cottage, enjoying his Havana, I am glad to learn from one of his intimate friends that the stories told of the President's excessive indulgence in whisky are " political exaggerations." Henry Clews, the banker, says he has never seen Grant "the worse for liquor;" that his favourite drink is champagne; and that he does not indulge over-freely in that comparatively harmless beverage. Regard for the high office he holds, which men of all parties and all nations entertain, makes this a very welcome fact. Justice to the President should be the maxim, even of his enemies.

ELECTRICITY.

ILL health, intense heat, "Indians on the war-path," detain me in New York equally against my wishes and my will. But no one in this world is a "free agent." Therefore *il faut être résigné.* In regard to health, the first of all blessings, fifty-five Turkish and Electric baths are telling favourably. As for the heat, when the mercury touches 102° in the shade, locomotion is irksome, not to say dangerous. "Sunstrokes" are daily increasing the catalogue of mortality. Suicides are also of frequent occurrence, no doubt owing to fever of the brain caused by the torrid atmosphere and the general collapse of the nervous system. And yet for the last two weeks scarcely a day has passed without terrific thunder-showers, which seem to hang over us for an hour or two for the express purpose of hurling their fiery bolts upon the devoted city. Not even in the tropics have I ever witnessed such awful exhibitions of electric combustion as during the last two weeks. Even at this instant, mid-day, the sheet on which I write is momently illuminated by fitful flashes of lightning, while "the rain falls in torrents, and the thunder rolls deep." My old reverence for Electricity, the Prime Minister of the Almighty, increases every hour. Night before last a "spark" fell, seeming as large as the sun, into the great Oil Tanks of Weehaken, at the Erie Railway station, opposite New York, and suddenly millions of gallons were in flame. The explosion was terrific; and the illumination, with a dense, jet-black cloud of smoke for background, was indescribably grand. This fearful calamity was eagerly used by the "Bears" to depress Erie, but on the official announcement that the Company's insurance exceeded their losses, the stock went up instead of down. Poor Bears! they remind me of the satirical old distich on the medical doctor—

> "Like Death himself, unhappy elf,
> He lives by others dying."

I have spoken of Electricity as the dread destroyer of life, and as the gentle restorer of life—as a Power to be both feared and adored. Omnipotent as this power appears to us, it is destined to be the slave, and not the master, of man. The lightning of heaven yielded to the philosophy of Franklin when he sent up his kite in the midst

of the tempest, drew the electric fluid from the
cloud, and "bottled up the thunder."

> "'Twas Franklin who first caught the horse,
> 'Twas harnessed by Professor Morse."

And now, "swift as thoughts of love," it has become the world's messenger at everybody's command. In the coming generations it will supersede all coarser elements for producing light, heat, and locomotion, and take the place of both doctor and druggist as healer of the sick. As yet the power and the uses of Electricity are but little understood. Millions of men in all ages of the world have naturally and devoutly worshipped the Sun, as the brightest and grandest representative of Creative Power. Science teaches us that the Sun himself, and the whole infinite system of suns, are but the visible, atomic manifestations of their Great Electric Cause—that subtle, omnipotent, Thought which we have reverently called the Prime Minister of the Deity. Consider this new and marvellous discovery just announced in America. Musical melodies transmitted over electric wires a distance of 2400 miles, and reproduced, note for note, on a violin, or any other suitable instrument! The time is near, we are assured, when messages across seas and continents will be sent *viva voce* without the use of any interlocutory apparatus. Even now there are telegraphic experts in New York whose ears are so acute that they can tell us the name of the person who is operating at the other end of the line, thousands of miles distant, by the peculiarity of touch or "click." It has become a common thing for Wall Street operators to go into a telegraph-station and ask to have a friend called to the station in Washington, when a conversation may be carried on for hours, without a written word passing between them. "I have had half-an-hour's chat with our friend Col. X. to-day," said a friend to me yesterday. "I thought he was in San Francisco," was my reply. "So he is; but I sent for him to come to the telegraph-office there, and we monopolised the wire, until an important operation in wheat was made, by which, after selling by cable to deliver in Liverpool, I have made 50,000 dollars, thanks to the telegraph." Who would have believed a prophecy to this effect twenty-five years ago? And yet we are only beginning to learn the alphabet of science, especially the mysteries of—

> "That electric chain
> Wherewith we are darkly bound."

Spiritualism, or moral electricity, is receiving a new impetus just now in New York from the presence of a Mr Brown, "the thought-reader."

This extraordinary public "Medium," who is giving illustrations of his miraculous talent, will find any article, no matter where or how occultly hidden, by placing the hand of the person who hid it on his own forehead, and, by this connection, reading the secret. Perhaps Dr Lynn, of the Egyptian Hall, could tell us "how it is done." But the people here "don't see it." Why not employ Brown as detective for the recovery of stolen goods? He professes to be able to read a murderer's thoughts, when he can get hold of one, and give all the details in regard to the victim. Why not submit the Beecher case to this infallible test? With the Parson's hand on the "Medium's" brow there might be a revelation as conclusive as that made by the guilty Queen in the "play scene" of "Hamlet." What will be the effect on Society when it comes to this that finely-organised men and women can read each other's thoughts "like books," may be more easily imagined than described. In the meantime, we are compelled to believe that there is *one* mind in the universe, if not more, that can read our thoughts as easily as we read our alphabet. Let us drop these abstrusities, and quit fancies for facts. On Saturday, the 11th of July, no less than six steamships left New York for Liverpool, Glasgow, and Plymouth, taking out about one thousand first-class passengers. The new *Britannic*, of the White Star Line, had every berth occupied, and was accompanied down the Bay by a large crowd of friends and admirers. The *Britannic* has made a great sensation in New York; and, like a belle at a ball, she is fully engaged a long way ahead. That is, from this side. Two classes of people are going to Europe for the summer, instead of to the watering-places at home —pleasure-seekers, and merchants engaged in foreign trade. The latter generally take their families, or two or three of them at least. This increasing international intercourse produces only good results on both sides of the Atlantic. These gigantic steamers, flying to and fro between Europe and America, like shuttles in a loom, are weaving the nations closer and closer together. Trade is benefited, opinions are modified, manners are improved, and minds are expanded and cosmopolitanised. Yes, travel is the very best means of education; and yet something besides travel is essential to that *rara avis in terris*, a "finished" gentleman or lady.

> "A man may have studied and travelled abroad,
> May sing like Apollo, and paint like a Claud,
> May speak all the languages under the Pole,
> And have every gift in the world but a Soul."

GRANT.

THIRD-TERM talk is a chimera of the New York *Herald;* a mere scarecrow set up as a target for the sharpshooters of the Press to practise on. As yet Grant has not given any public intimation of a desire to extend his Administration from eight years to twelve, and I have yet to find the politician or journalist who has openly and clearly declared himself in favour of a third-term candidate. The whole people are opposed to it as a violation of an unwritten clause in the Constitution. Washington, Adams, Jefferson, and all the early Presidents deprecated a third-term election as a dangerous consolidation of executive powers, and a preliminary step towards despotism. Perhaps the very best thing Congress could do, *before* the Presidential election of 1876, would be to extend the term from four years to eight, or ten, and prohibit re-election. This would tend to elevate the Administration above all party influences and considerations, while relieving the country from the quadrennial debauch of a Presidential campaign. It would also ensure a more settled policy in Federal legislation. As a new House is to be elected in the coming autumn, this question of extending the Presidential term demands immediate attention. Although Grant is silent as a sphinx on the subject, it is by no means certain that he is not contemplating a new lease of power. It would, no doubt, be regarded by this "happy accident" of political ambition as a "big thing" to beat his illustrious predecessors in the White House by four years, while, for the greater portion of the period, enjoying a doubled salary. Besides, the most sanguine Republicans appear to give up all hope of electing any other candidate *but* Grant. This consideration may compel his re-nomination. Mr Speaker Blaine, who is about the only Republican spoken of as Grant's successor, is an extreme New Englander, with not the least chance of success. On the Democratic side there are several "Richmonds in the field;" but the big potatoes will only come to the top after the jolting of the Fall elections. At this present writing Senator Thurman, of Ohio, looms up largest, and, so far as talent and character are concerned, Mr Thurman deserves to be regarded as Chief of the Conservative party. Thurman and Lamar would make a strong ticket.

But I will venture no more political forecastings to-day. I have just been told who will succeed Mr Jewell as Minister at St Petersburg, but I promised not to tell. I am authorised, however, to state that it will not be ex-Senator Nye, nor an ex-Confederate General, although the former is urged by Silver Senator Jones of Nevada, and the latter is a bosom friend of Grant. Senator Jones, by the way, is now a guest at the "Everett House," and, with his snug little income of 250,000 dollars a month, has no end of "friends." But for the unfortunate accident of being a born Englishman, the silver-coated Senator would stand a good chance of becoming President of the United States. The Constitution makes American nativity a *sine qua non* qualification for the Presidency; although certain heretic writers contend that George Washington was born in England, while Andrew Jackson's Irish emigrant mother arrived only just in time to save him from being debarred by the alien law. In a recent article we noticed the conspicuous absence of great men in the present Senate of the United States. Almost an equal degeneration may be found both in the profession of literature and in the ranks of journalism. In our own day we have personally known and admired such world-famous editors as Bennett, of the *Herald;*

Greeley, of the *Tribune;* Raymond, of the *Times;* Croswell, of the *Argus;* Ritchie, of the *Union;* Gales, of the *Intelligencer;* Prentice, of the Louisville *Journal,* &c., &c. "All are gone, the old familiar faces." And whom have we left worthily to fill their places? Bryant, of the *Post;* Brooks, of the *Express;* and who can name another? There are, no doubt, many good writers now connected with the American Press, but none of striking individuality, who stand out in bold relief, like the veteran knights of the quill we have named, who filled the field of journalism during the last quarter of a century. As for American poets and novelists, they seem to be rapidly diminishing, both in number and in celebrity. After Longfellow, the American Tennyson; Bryant, the minstrel of the Past; and Joaquin Miller, the Swinburne of the West, what American poet is there to-day that commits himself to memory? Even N. P. Willis, as a writer of *vers de société,* has left no successor. In the graver field of historical lore, America may boast of two living writers second to none in Europe—Bancroft and Motley. The latter we do not hesitate to pronounce the greatest historian of the age. A thorough scholar, an accomplished gentleman—none but a gentleman can write pure classics—Motley's works are more truly monumental than anything in the way of literature the New World has yet produced. I have not forgotten in this category Prescott and Irving, the pure historian, and the delightful essayist and biographer. Among the humorists, or funnygraphers of the day, America rejoices in three who have suddenly risen to the top wave of popularity—Mark Twain, Bret Harte, and John Hay. As an illustration of how this talent called wit pays, it is announced that Mark Twain has built a 100,000 dollars' villa, Bret Harte receives 500 dollars for a one-page story in the *Times*, written at a sitting, and Hay has " possessed himself" of a precious stone worth several millions.

SARATOGA.

The eyes and the thoughts of young America, masculine and feminine, have been concentrated on Saratoga during the past week. On the 16th of July the Intercollegiate Regatta was announced to come off on Saratoga Lake, a beautiful sheet of water, about three miles from the " Springs," which seems to have been expressly prepared for pleasure purposes. Nine colleges entered for the race, and we will name them in the order in which they passed the " stake boat "—Columbia, Wesleyan, Harvard, Williams, Cornell, Dartmouth, Princeton, Trinity, Yale. The rowing Regatta is a new " institution " on this side of the Atlantic; and, like the principles of *Magna Charta*, and many other good things, is imported from England. Judging from the universal interest, I may say intense excitement, caused by this rowing match, we may well conclude that Boating has already become the most popular item in the *curriculum* of American college " exercises." A few facts in connection with this contest will best illustrate the *furore* it has created. The famous *Spa*, known as Saratoga Springs, I must inform European readers, is situated some 180 miles north of New York, and for the last half-century it has been the grand resort of health and pleasure seekers from all parts of the Union; but the " season " is brief, lasting only from the 1st of July to the 1st of September. Within the last decade Saratoga has added to its natural attractions of pure air and medicinal waters such artificial stimulants as horse-racing, boat-racing, and card-gambling. In these fascinating concomitants of advanced civilisation, the place has become almost as bewitchingly wicked as the delightful " Hells " of Homburg, Baden, and Monaco. But in the still more dangerous accessories of what Paris now calls " cocottes, or Ladies of the Lake," Saratoga is simply " nowhere." It is ironically said that these inverted angels would stand no chance here in competition with the more respectable or " honest " class of women. But I do not believe a word of it. I did not see or hear anything in all this vast assemblage that was in the slightest degree shocking, improper, or unvirtuous ; and why should we ever be so uncharitable as to infer the existence thereof? But I suppose in this, as in all things else, " he that seeketh findeth "

—and findeth *what* he seeketh. The glorious old Hudson, or North River, has not changed in all these changeful years, only its banks have become dotted with villages, and embroidered with villas. Although the majestic stream is perpetually emptying itself into the beautiful Bay of New York, yet the full fresh flood seems always the same, while the tide still ebbs and flows with the long and lazy pulsation of the sea. Is it the mystic influence of the moon, or the diurnal motion of the earth, that causes this mathematical movement of the waters? The latter, no doubt. We left the hot city on Tuesday evening, the 14th of July, at six o'clock, in the immense and really magnificent steamer *St John* for Albany. The Regatta was advertised for the 16th, and from all parts of the country, and all points of the compass, the tide of travel was rushing towards the Springs. Our "floating palace" carried nearly two thousand passengers, all "first class," but of a most motley mixture. When fairly out in the stream, a delicious moist-winged breeze came down the River, fanning the panting crowd into a mood of momentary happiness. People are always amiable, and generally gay, when suddenly relieved from suffering. I have known the most morose men to dance on having a tooth out, on hearing of a mother-in-law's departure for a better world, or any other stroke of good fortune that "put them out of misery." And so when the cool of the evening came waltzing down from the Highlands, our happy little party partook of the general joy. Yonkers, a few miles up the River, which we knew almost before it wore trousers, is now a considerable city, planted in the midst of a forest. Barring the mosquitoes, if there are any of those intolerable little bores there, no town in the vicinity of New York looks more inviting than this same Yonkers with its awkward, gawky name. Why not do as young ladies sometimes do—change it? Speaking of mosquitoes, I will confess to a little weakness. On hearing the old familiar music of these devoted serenaders for the first time in many years—the tune has not varied in the least—the same monotonous cry for blood—I was overcome for a moment by sad and painful reminiscences. I remembered all the battles I had fought from childhood up with this diminutive but most formidable enemy, and recalled the child's puzzling question—"Mamma, you say nothing is made in vain. What were mosquitoes made for?" And mamma, I am sorrow to say, never gave a satisfactory answer to the earnest inquiry. English readers can hardly realise that these almost invisible insects make certain localities in this country uninhabitable during certain months of the year, and the first question I would advise an emigrant to settle before settling himself in any particular spot in America, is the all-important mosquito question. Grasshopper and locust devastations are terrible calamities, but nothing in comparison to the visitation of the mosquito bore, which means, " sleep no more " to all the house. I have already confessed to a little touch of sentimentality on hearing the first mosquito chant his welcome home after so long an absence; but the enemy greatly outnumbers me; fighting is useless; and I feel inclined to beat a hasty retreat out of the enemy's country. England, with all her faults, has no mosquitoes. After passing a few restless hours in one of the *St John's* numberless " Bridal State-rooms," with its spacious and sumptuous bed, " not made for slumber," we reached Albany, the State capital, 150 miles from New York, at five o'clock A.M., and at seven o'clock took the cars for Saratoga, arriving at half-past nine o'clock. And here was a transformation scene indeed! Four new hotels, capable of accommodating an aggregate of 6000 guests, with their beautiful gardens, seem to have crowded everything out of town, occupying the whole space of the old village. With rooms engaged in advance at the " United States," the newest and the grandest of all these grand hotels, the long *queue* at "the office" of ardent room-seekers did not alarm us. Breakfast was ready, and so were we. The dining-room covers half an acre, seats 1000 persons at table, who are received by an army of 200 "coloured gentlemen," but not, as formerly, dressed in the cool, clean white linen uniform. Considering that the hotel had just been opened, that its forces had not had sufficient time for organisation and drill, and that there were no less than 1500 persons to room and feed, the administration was wonderfully efficient and generally satisfactory. The "United States" occupies the site of the old hotel of the same name, which was destroyed by fire nine years ago, and the phœnix that has recently risen from the ashes, at a cost of a million of dollars, is hailed by the public as a favourite work revised, and improved in type, and greatly enlarged in margin. There is no watering-place hotel that I have seen, or heard of, either in Europe or America, that equals it in size, accommodation, and comfort. Saratoga has one principal street, Broadway, on which the hotel has a frontage of 230 feet. It is built in the form of a hollow parallelogram, the sides extending 715 feet, embracing a garden, handsomely laid out in walks, and lined with trees and plants. When enlivened with playing fountains, and illuminated with gas jets, the garden of the "United States" will look as gay as a little *Mabille*. There are 768 sleeping-rooms, besides 65 suites, each of which has from one to seven connecting rooms, with baths, &c. The dining-hall measures 212 by 52 feet, with a ceiling of 26 feet; has eight chandeliers, which, with the 38 side-brackets, give a total of 276 burners. The drawing-room is 87 by 50; ceiling, 26 feet; has 14 windows, and 75 gas-burners. It is most elaborately furnished in blue, gold, and water-coloured silks, with heavy lambrequins of light-blue silk. The furniture of this room cost 20,000 dollars. The ball-room is 112 by 52 feet; has three chandeliers, 83 burners, and 30 windows. The Enunciator is 20 feet in height, and cost 10,000 dollars. It registers 916 rooms. The carpets were furnished by A. T. Stewart & Co. The parlour carpet is an Axminster of 500 yards, and cost four dollars per yard. There are two passenger elevators in the hotel. The piazzas measure 2700 feet in length, and the lawn covers three acres, on the south margin of which are located 63 hotel cottages. The firm which manages this magnificent establishment is Ainsworth, Perry, Tompkins, & Co. Mr Marvin, who has been connected with the hotel business in Saratoga since 1830, and who for some years represented the district in

Congress, is the principal stockholder in the new concern, and still keeps his eye on the management from the force of habit; while Major Field, who has been the popular "room clerk" of the hotel ever since he was three feet high, is still at his post, with pen behind his ear, and the same cordial "glad to see you" on his lips. The sewage and "w. c." improvements of the "United States," a matter of fundamental importance, hitherto shamefully overlooked in Saratoga hotels, are worthy of all praise. But we are a long time in getting to the Regatta, which, by the way, I shall leave to the sporting papers to describe. It was announced to take place at 4 P.M. on the 16th, and not less than 20,000 people, perhaps twice this number, gathered on the borders of the Lake as eager spectators of the contest. Owing to a little roughness of the surface of the water, the race was postponed until the following day at five o'clock, and again postponed, for the same reason, until the third day at ten A.M., when the "event" actually took place, but in presence of a greatly diminished crowd of "assistants." The result was a general disappointment; at the same time, it created a whirlwind of rejoicing, Columbia—the New York City College crew—having only taken to the water within the last two years. There was a great deal of betting on the match; even the

New York Stock Exchange suspended the regular business for pool transactions on the Regatta. The "fouling," and consequent unpleasantness between Harvard and Yale, were the only clouds in this brilliant *fête*. The moral effect of all this excitement I do not propose to discuss; but leave that to parents, guardians, and college professors. No doubt "muscular Christianity" is a good thing; but the habit of betting is not a good thing. There is also a possibility of over-training and over-straining. One of the rowers in the victorious boat fainted on passing the winning-point, and had to be carried ashore. I cannot leave the Regatta without contributing my modicum of thanks to Mr and Mrs Frank Leslie—who, by the way, were united in holy wedlock last week —for the generous hospitality extended to a large number of friends at their charming Swiss cottage —" Interlaken "—on the border of the Lake, from which we enjoyed a " proscenium " view of the whole performance in a large and pleasant company of distinguished persons, including Mrs Ann S. Stephens, the authoress; Hon. Fernando Wood, Hon. Augustus Schell, George Francis Train, W. H. Vanderbilt, and many others not unknown to fame. The grand Balls, in commemoration of the "event," simultaneously in motion at the four great hotels, commenced at six P.M. on Saturday, and closed at midnight, the good orthodox Saratogans not daring, as in Paris and other cosmopolitan cities, to borrow a few hours of the Lord on Sunday morning. The difficulty, however, might have been got over by stopping the clock before twelve. The daily papers of the following Monday were largely occupied in descriptions of the belles, and the items and fashions of their toilettes. As the clothes line is not exactly in mine, I will only quote one or two " cases " from other journals, and these only because they are *Cosmopolitan* subscribers, and therefore deserve especial recognition. Among the young belles, the rising stars of American society, none sparkled more brilliantly than Sue Train, the only daughter of George Francis, who was " engaged ahead " for dances enough to last through the season. As this gifted and accomplished young lady is a special pet of the *Presidente* of our " Ladies' Club," there was more than one wish expressed that " The Countess " could have been present to have sketched this graceful *Train* in motion. But the father's constant devotion to his beautiful " photograph," like a blacksmith's leather apron, keeps off the " sparks ; " and Mdlle Sue-belle, with her *exigeant* standard of manhood, will not be easily suited. The next on our list is Mrs Judge Smith, a charming matron of Chicago, long resident in Europe, and a thorough cosmopolitan. The gems she wears, and the "jewels" that follow in her train, three sons and one daughter, make her presence everywhere luminous and delightful, while the smiling partner of all her joys and treasures makes every one he meets happy by the magnetic grasp of his cordial and generous hand. Another cosmopolitan belle is thus "touched up" by the *Herald:*—" Mrs O. H. Blood, of New York, one of the belles of the ball, was dressed in rich white gros grain, the train trimmed with plaited ruffles of the same material, and the front braid arranged in puffs; a white blonde overdress, caught up with clusters of roses; low corsage and short sleeves, trimmed with lace in plaits. She wore rich diamonds, and her hair was arranged in chatelain braids, with clusters of curls, looking very becoming." In naming the celebrities at Saratoga, it might be deemed a little invidious if no mention was made of the presence of Commodore Vanderbilt, Jay Gould, and President Grant. Mr Gould happened to be seated near me in a " Drawing-room " car down to New York. He is a small, sharp, dark, bright-eyed man, who can "see" his antagonist's game, and "go him better" quicker than any other gambler in Wall

Street. He does not look more than forty years of age; but men of his "calling" sometimes live years in minutes, and grow old very fast. Vanderbilt has "lived" more in eighty years than most men would in a hundred and sixty.

BEECHER.

The newspapers of the day are again filled with the "Beecher Scandal," the formal, circumstantial, *sworn* statement of Theodore Tilton, and everybody is discussing the comparative merits of saints and sinners. So far as my own experience of the world goes, the greatest saints are the greatest sinners, simply because, while arrogating to themselves all the virtues, they practise, under the garb of sanctity, all the vices of humanity. Men who boast of having "got" religion, as if it were something in the shape of a first-class railway ticket to heaven, are never to be trusted. The very profession is a falsehood and a fraud. An honest man, one who will not lie to save, I will not say his soul, but his fortune—a man of integrity and of honour has all the "religion" necessary for this world, or any other. Such a man would not steal his friend's purse, much less the affections of his friend's wife, even though he belonged to no "church," and was denounced by all the saints as a "wicked man of the world." "You are very beautiful and sorely tempting," said Joseph to Mrs Potiphar, "but you are the consecrated wife of one who calls me his friend, and confides in my honour. You would despise me if I were to rob your husband's bank, and assist by your testimony in sending me to prison. How much more should I despise myself if I were to rob him of his wife's honour, the 'immediate jewel of the soul!'" We are not quoting the words of the Rev. Artemus Ward Beecher, addressed to the wife of his dear friend Tilton; only the words that every honourable "sinner" would use under the trying circumstances. Without going into the repulsive details of this infamous story of "religious" seduction, we cannot altogether ignore a revelation that brings out in bold relief "the devil's pet sin, hypocrisy." The New York *Tribune* says—" Unless this frightful exposition is answered promptly and fully, the most famous pulpit the world has ever seen since Paul preached on the Hill of Mars is silenced, the life of the greatest preacher in the world is ended. It is useless to fall back upon the record of a spotless and glorious career. There is no longer safety or dignity in the proud silence which would have so well become the great pastor if there were no words of his own to be explained." We do not agree with the *Tribune* in regard to Beecher's "greatness." Eccentricity is not greatness. Beecher is certainly a man of talent, and of cultivation, and in this respect he may even outrank the preacher of Mars Hill. But he is simply a pulpit orator and actor, always speaking and posing for effect. All his sermons and speeches are pregnant with "amativeness." Hence full houses, and a revenue of 50,000 dollars a year. Beecher for thirty years has lived the life of a Sybarite, and knows nothing practically of the self-sacrificing doctrines of Christianity. He is simply a "pious fraud," and no man knows it better than himself. And this is more or less true of all the "saints" of the I-am-holier-than-thou persuasion. The last time I saw his Reverence he was sitting in the Champs Elysées, with a very red face, beside a pretty cocotte, and a glass in his hand that, destined to any "sinner's" lips, would have naturally and honestly passed for a glass of "B. and S." Mr Theodore Tilton's statement of his charges and proof against Mr Beecher, as read to the Committee of Beecher's particular friends, has been published. It is, in terms, a specific allegation of adultery, committed by Mr Beecher with Mrs Tilton, first at Mr Beecher's own house on the evening of October 10, 1868, and frequently thereafter at the resid-

ences of both, and elsewhere, until the spring of
1870. It alleges Mr Tilton's discovery of Mr
Beecher locked up with Mrs Tilton in her bedroom; his seeing improper liberties taken with
her by Mr Beecher in his library; Mrs Tilton's
own confession to him of her guilt, and her explanations of it, on July 3, 1870; that this confession was subsequently put in writing by her,
and was shown by Mr F. D. Moulton to Mr
Beecher; that Mr Beecher first procured from
Mrs Tilton a written retraction of the whole
story, and then confessed to Mr Moulton his own
guilt, returned to the latter Mrs Tilton's retraction, and threatened suicide in case of exposure.
The full text of Mr Beecher's apology is given,
with parts of several other letters by him, addressed, like it, to Mr Moulton, all expressing
remorse and contrition for some great but unnamed
wrong done Mr and Mrs Tilton. A letter from
Mr Beecher to Mr Tilton eulogises Moulton as the
friend who had tied up the storm ready to burst
on their heads. A letter from Mrs Tilton to her
husband, naming no one, says she first saw that
the love she felt and received was sinful on reading "Griffith Gaunt," and assures her husband
now of a purified and restored love whenever he
turns towards her with true feeling. The latter
part of the statement deals with the provocations

given for this exposure by both Mr Moulton and
Mr Tilton; and with the happiness and quiet of
the family life thus destroyed for ever. We have
little respect for poor Tilton, notwithstanding the
cruel wrong he has received from the " Pastor "
whom he worshipped, the priest who married him,
and the " friend " who offered to " share with
him his fortune." Once satisfied of the terrible
fact, Tilton should either have killed Beecher or
quit his wife. If there is any sincerity in Beecher's
"longing for death," this would have been the
greatest possible favour to the Seducer. The following letter is the cry of a guilty conscience,
after the crime is detected.

"MY DEAR FRIEND MOULTON,—I ask, through you, Theodore
Tilton's forgiveness, and I humble myself before him as I do
before my God. He would have been a better man in my
circumstances than I have been. I can ask nothing, except
that he will remember all the other breasts that would ache.
I will not plead for myself. I even wish that I were dead.
But others must live to suffer. I will die before any one but
myself shall be inculpated. All my thoughts are running out
toward my friends, and toward the poor child lying there, and
praying with her folded hands. She is guiltless, sinned
against, bearing the transgression of another. Her forgiveness
I have. I humbly pray to God to put it into the heart of her
husband to forgive me. I have trusted this to Moulton in
confidence. H. W. BEECHER."

An innocent man, falsely calumniated, is bold,
proud, defiant, and does not drop on his knees

whimpering for " forgiveness." The next letter is addressed to Mrs Tilton by her husband's permission :—

"BROOKLYN, *February* 7, 1871.

"MY DEAR MRS TILTON,—When I saw you last, I did not expect ever to see you again, or to be alive many days. God was kinder to me than were my own thoughts. The friend whom God sent to me, Mr Moulton, has proved, above all friends that I ever had, able and willing to help me in this terrible emergency of my life. His hand it was that tied up the storm that was ready to burst on our heads. You have no friend (Theodore excepted) who has it in his power to serve you so vitally, and who will do it with such delicacy and honour. It does my sore heart good to see in Mr Moulton an unfeigned respect and honour for you. It would kill me if I thought otherwise. He will be as true a friend to your honour and happiness as a brother could be to a sister's. In him we have a common ground. You and I may meet in him. The past is ended. But is there no future? No wiser, higher, holier future? May not this friend stand as a priest in the new sanctuary of reconciliation, and mediate and bless Theodore and my most unhappy self? Do not let my earnestness fail of its end. You believe in my judgment. I have put myself wholly and gladly in Moulton's hand. And there I must meet you. This is sent with Theodore's consent, but he has not read it. Will you return it to me by his own hand? I am very earnest in this wish, for all our sakes, as such a letter ought not to be submitted to even a chance of miscarriage.—Your unhappy friend, H. W. BEECHER."

The following letter to Moulton is full of confession, especially in what may be read between the lines :—

"*February* 7, 1871.

"MY DEAR FRIEND MOULTON,—I am glad to send you a book, &c. ... Many, many friends has God raised up to me, but to no one of them has He ever given the opportunity and the wisdom so to serve me as you have. You have also proved Theodore's friend and Elizabeth's. Does God look down from heaven on three unhappier creatures that more need a friend than these ? Is it not an intimation of God's intent of mercy to all that each one of these has in you a tried and proved friend ? But only in you are we thus united. Would to God, who orders all hearts, that by His kind mediation Theodore, Elizabeth, and I could be made friends again. Theodore will have the hardest task in such a case ; but has he not proved himself capable of the noblest things ? I wonder if Elizabeth knows how generously he has carried himself toward me. Of course I can never speak with her again without his permission, and I do not know that even then it would be best. . . . ."

To show the feeling entertained by Mrs Heloise Tilton towards her Abelard before the " pastoral visits " and " nest hiding " game of her seducer, we quote the following warm and gushing effusions :—

" *Tuesday Morning, January* 28, 1868.

" My Beloved,—Don't you know the peculiar phase of Christ's character as a lover is so precious to me because of my consecration and devotion to you ? I learn to love you from my love to Him. Nor do I feel one whit irreverent. And as every day I adorn myself, consciously, as a bride to meet her bridegroom, so in like manner I lift imploring hands that my soul's love may be prepared. I, with the little girls, after you left us, with overflowing eyes and hearts, consecrated ourselves to our work and to you. My waking thoughts last night were of you. My rising thoughts this morning were of you. I bless you ; I honour you ; I love you. God sustain us, and help us both to keep our vows."

"*Saturday Evening, February* 1, 1868.
"Oh! well I know, as far as I am capable, I love you. Now to keep this fire high and generous is the ideal before me. I am only perfectly contented and restful when you are with me. These latter months I have thought, looked, and yearned for the hour when you would be at home with longings unutterable."

"*Monday, February* 3, 1868—9 *o'clock* A.M.
"What may I bring to my beloved this bright morning? A large throbbing heart full of love, single in its aim and purpose to bless and cheer him? Is it acceptable, sweet one?"

"*Monday Morning, February* 24, 1868.
" Do you wonder that I couple your love, your presence, and relation to me with the Saviour's? I lift you up sacredly, and keep you in that exalted and holy place where I reverence, respect, and love, with the fervency of my whole being. Whatever capacity I have, I offer it to you. The closing lines of your letter are these words—'I shall hardly venture again upon a great friendship—your love shall be enough for the remaining days.' That word 'enough' seems a stoicism on which you have resolved to live your life—but I pray God He will supply you with friendships pure, and with wifely love which your great heart demands, withholding not Himself as the Chief Love which consumeth not though it burn, and whose effects are always perfect rest and peace. Again, in one of your letters you close with 'Faithfully yours'—that word Faithful means a great deal. Yes, darling, I believe it, trust it and give you the same surety with regard to myself. I am faithful to you, have been always, and shall for ever be, world without end. Call not this assurance impious; there are some things we know. Blessed be God."

"*Home, February* 29, 1868—*Saturday Evening.*
"Ah! did ever man ever love so grandly as my Beloved? Other friendships, public affairs, all 'fall to nought' when I come to you. Though you are in Dacotah to-night, yet I have felt your love, and am very grateful for it. I had not received a

line since Monday, and was so hungry and lonesome, that I took out all your letters and indulged myself as at a feast, but without satiety. And now I long to pour out into your heart of my abundance. I am conscious of three jets to the fountain of my soul—to the Great Lover and yourself—to whom as one I am eternally wedded; my children; and the dear friends who trust and love me. I do not want another long separation. While we are in the flesh let us abide together."

"*Saturday Morning, March* 1868.

"Oh, how almost perfectly could I minister to you this winter, my heart glows so perpetually! I am conscious of great inward awakening toward you. If I live, I shall teach my children to begin their loves where now I am. I cannot conceive of anything more delicious than a life consecrated to a faithful love. I insist that I miss you more than you do me, but soon I shall see my beloved.

"YOUR OWN DEAR WIFE."

And the " dear wife," who dipped her pen in her heart when writing the above, is now in "battle array" against her own Theodore, adding the crime of perjury to the sin of adultery, in order to save Plymouth Church and its "popular pastor!" O frailty, thy name is—Elizabeth! Here let us pass the great " Religious Scandal" over to the judgment of history, which, in the end, is sure to be just. The minor sensations of the day are the kidnapping of a four-year-old boy in Philadelphia, and the "boy murderer" in Boston. In the former heartrending outrage the child-thieves are negotiating through the Press with the agonised parents for the surrender of the boy, 20,000 dollars having been raised for the ransom. The city should offer at least 100,000 dollars for the arrest of the perpetrators of the atrocious crime. Jesse Pomeroy, the boy brute, who murdered little Katie Curran from pure "cussedness," is the lion of Boston. He is the son of a butcher, and the amiable theory has been started that he inherited the love of killing, and that the natural propensity is irresistible. But the mother of the young monster has come out with a denial of the inherited theory, and says his father was not actually a butcher of animals, but only served the dead meat. She also publishes a statement that will be "nuts" to our anti-vaccination friends. We quote from Mrs Pomeroy's letter to the Boston journals :—" I have frequently received letters from persons in all parts of the country, principally in the West, asking for some of Jesse's hair, and other absurd requests, that I have not paid any attention to. The story of Jesse sticking knives into raw flesh is also false. I think his vaccination had more effect on him than anything else. He was vaccinated when he was four weeks old, and shortly after his face broke out, and had the appearance of raw flesh, and some fluid issued from the wounds that burned my arm when it dropped on it, from which fact I judged the fluid was poison. This lasted until he was six months old, when his whole body was covered with abscesses, one of which was over his eye, and occasioned the cast or fallen appearance that he wears at present. At the time it was thought he would die, but he recovered slowly, and Dr Lane, who attended him, stated that all the sickness was occasioned by vaccination." After this, let those who will vaccinate their children; but against the law that makes this disgusting superstition "compulsory" we feel it our duty to stoutly and persistently rebel.

PROVIDENCE.

It was a tedious ten hours' rail-ride from Stephentown, N.Y., to Boston; but one that I shall not soon forget, on account of a most murderous accident that happened to a fellow-passenger. Accident is not the word for the atrocity I am about to relate. Just before arriving at the Palmer Station, between Springfield and Worcester, a sharp, jagged stone, about the size of a man's fist, was hurled with great force through the left front window of the car, inflicting a fearful, if not fatal, wound on the head of a lady sitting directly in front of me. A deep gash was made in the scalp about an inch above the temple, from which the blood flowed profusely over the lady and the infant in her arms. At the same instant a still larger stone was thrown into the smoking-car forward, also badly wounding a gentleman in the head. Both victims were left at the station, the lady in a state of insensibility On the succeeding evening, when that same train, the Albany and Boston Express, was approaching

the same station, a rail was discovered across the
track, which, not being fastened, was thrown off
by the "cow-catcher." A large reward has been
offered by the Railway Company for these repeated
outrages, and one or two vagabonds have been
arrested on suspicion. It is a singular coincidence
that this same train, in charge of the same con-
ductor, was fired into near Natick some two months
ago, and a gentleman sitting near me when the
lady was hit most narrowly escaped the bullet of
the indiscriminate assassin. I will relate another
incident in connection with this affair, for the special
gratification of superstitious believers in "signs
and warnings." When this lady, predestined to
be wounded, entered the car at Springfield, she
was accompanied by her husband, a little girl of
about three years, and an infant of, perhaps, as
many months. Among the luggage brought into
the car was a large looking-glass, which was placed
upright in the corner, in front of the family party.
Soon after leaving the station, by a sudden lurch
of the car the looking-glass fell with a crash,
breaking into a thousand pieces, which seemed
greatly to disconcert the young wife, and to cause
an animated conversation on the subject with her
husband. At the very moment the missile struck
the poor lady senseless, I was "wondering" what
accident would befall the party in consequence of

this small calamity. And I am *not* superstitious. Fifteen years ago, in travelling by rail through a dense forest in South Carolina in a pitch-dark night, in company with Charles Mackay, the poet, as we were sitting side by side, a bullet crashed through the window and whizzed before our noses. But this bullet had not its "billet" for either of us. No accident can forestall destiny; and, admitting God's omniscience—and without omniscience God is not infinite—each man's exit from the world is just as fixed as his entrance. This "belief" is denounced as "fatalism." It is simply absolute faith and confidence in the Deity, a perfect faith that "casteth out fear." All along through Massachusetts the country has become populous with villages, while the large towns are doubling every ten years, and nearly all the land is under cultivation. Although only settled 250 years, the "Old Bay State" really begins to look like an old country. Pittsfield, Springfield, Worcester, have grown into places of great wealth and importance, and the cheering word *thrift* is written on farms, fences, houses, and manufactories all the way from Berkshire to Bunker's Hill. In no State are the various industries which make up the wealth and happiness of a people cultivated more thoroughly, economically, and intelligently, than in the Mother State of the Union by the descendants of the "Old

Colonies " of Plymouth, Salem, and Boston. " But
I shall offer no encomium on Massachusetts; there
she is, and there is her history." I found Boston
immensely expanded, and vastly improved by time,
fire, and reconstruction. But Webster, Everett,
Choate, Lawrence, Prescott, are no longer there
to gild the fair city with the lustre of their glorious names. Yet they "still live" in grateful
memories, and, like the immortal authors and
orators of Greece, crown our "modern Athens"
with the unfading halo of immortal genius. Boston
has something more than material wealth to boast
of. Of all New England towns Providence appears
to be the most substantially prosperous. Since
1840 the population of the city has quintupled,
having risen from 20,000 to 100,000, and the
wealth of the inhabitants has increased in, perhaps,
even a greater ratio. Nowhere have I met more
striking " transformation scenes " than in the once
familiar streets of the "City of Roger Williams,"
where, in 1836, when a very "young youth," I
wrote the "Anonymous Ode" commemorative of
the second centennial anniversary of the landing
of the Baptist pilgrim in Mooshasick, at the head
of Narragansett Bay, where the piously-named city
of Providence now stands. The Rev. Charles W.
Upham, of Salem, introduces this Ode in his
" Life of Roger Williams;" but the authorship,

I believe, has never before been publicly mentioned. It was set to music for the "patriotic occasion" by Professor Hansen, a Dane, then a celebrated teacher in Providence, and performed, under his direction, by the choir of the First Baptist Church. In now acknowledging the parentage of this offspring of youthful indiscretion, I may, without vanity, quote the words of Douglas Jerrold in reclaiming one of his stray intellectual children—"A small thing, but mine own." In walking up Westminster Street, where "Butler's Arcade" stands almost alone among the monuments of the past, the face of ex-Mayor Knight was the only one recognised, and that but dimly at first, among the fresh tide of life flowing up and down that well-worn and fashionable thoroughfare, devoted to business and promenade. In Green Street, where stood my little "Grecian Temple," dedicated by Ralph Waldo Emerson, and consecrated and graced by the teachings of Margaret Fuller and Georgina Nias, and where a charming nursery of the beautiful Spring buds and twigs of Providence, of both sexes, were carefully and tenderly unfolded and "bent," not a vestige remains of that garden of innocence and "seminary of learning." All those pretty little girls, not dead, are mothers now, some even grandmothers; while the lively little boys are transformed into grave bank presidents, eminent lawyers, rich manufacturers, distinguished authors, &c., &c., with grey whiskers and careworn faces. And the fathers and mothers of this new generation, where are they? One short, hard, sad word tells the story—dead. Such is the ever-flowing tide of human life: all go out with the ebb, and none return with the flood. And thus the world keeps ever young and fresh and new—

"Men may come and men may go,
But *life* flows on for ever."

Among the finest architectural improvements of Providence, the magnificent building opposite the "Arcade," erected by W. Butler Duncan, Esq., the wealthy New York banker, who is indebted to Providence for his fortune, stands out in bold relief. It compares favourably with the splendid "Drexel Building" in New York. The new Post-office is also a fine edifice; but there is another "going up" that has long been greatly needed—a first-class hotel. The foundations are being laid, covering a large area in Weybosset Street, adjoining the Opera House. It will cost half a million of dollars, and supply a real want, the city having long since outgrown all its old hotels. On both sides of the beautiful blue Narragansett Bay, new villages, cottages, towns, and watering-places have blossomed all the way from

Providence to Newport. The trip on board the steamer is a most delightful one, charming to the eye and exhilarating to the lungs. It is seldom that a traveller finds himself too soon at his journey's end; but we would gladly have extended the two hours between the two Rhode Island Capitals of Providence and Newport to ten. The bright blue Bay, reflecting the softer blue sky; the richly variegated shores, waving with the growing grain, and dotted with white homes where peace and plenty seem to dwell, make up one of those pleasant panoramas with which we hate to part, as from a charming " passing acquaintance." Rhode Island is one of the least of all the States in territory, but one of the greatest in all the elements essential to social and political happiness. Free from debt, free from pauperism, rich in agriculture and manufactures, with a salubrious climate, a school system unsurpassed, Newport for a summer resort, the Providence *Journal* for a daily newspaper, and its clever editor to represent them for life in the United States Senate, what more can a rational people desire! And this is Newport of blessed memory! We recognise the name of the town, its moist, cool atmosphere, that so quickly removes the dry varnish from the skin, and puts one to sleep like an anodyne; and also the old familiar faces of " Weaver," the excellent host, and " John,"

K

the venerable waiter, at "The Ocean." And that's
all. How the trees have grown, and the villas
multiplied during these fourteen years of absence,
while other lips and other eyes have sung the praise,
and feasted on the beauties of this sweet city by
the sea! I dare not indulge in reminiscences. It
was here that "Belle Brittan" made her *debut* in
the literary world, and so befogged and befooled
the critics who wrote love letters by the bushel to
the *fair incognita.* The "Ocean House" is not
crowded, the cottages take the cream of the visitors.
The hotel is greatly improved in many particulars;
but the old *habitués* are sadly missed, and the Band,
three times a day, treats us to the most melancholy
music, as if expressly devoted to dirges for the
Past. If the people now here feel gay they certainly have a sad way of showing it. "It is all owing
to the panic," I hear on every hand; but surely
the fearful "shrinkage" of last Autumn has not
made everybody bankrupt. It is estimated that
the loss on stocks in New York within the past
twelve months is over 200,000,000 dollars, and
that all second and third mortgages in real estate
in that city are "wiped out;" but most of these
Newport cottagers must be rich, nevertheless.
And, pray, why should they partake of the general gloom? There seems to be something in the
universal atmosphere that oppresses all classes of

society. Whether it is the "shrinkage" that has bursted thousands, who are not yet fully aware of the fact, or the fall of Beecher, which, like Sampson among the Philistines, is bringing down the pillars of the Christian temple, or a "fearful looking for of *judgments* to come," I do not know; but possibly it may be a combination of all these evil influences, together with the comet, that is making things, as Bill Nye, of Heathen-Chinee fame, in reply to the question, "How goes it, Truthful?" said, "It is far, far from gay." Altogether the most charming villa in Newport, considering location, stables, billiard-rooms, bowling alleys, bathing-houses, flower-gardens, &c., belongs to George Francis Train, designed, built, and furnished by his accomplished wife during her errant lord's confinement in an Irish Bastille. But the eccentric owner of this charming, costly place says he prefers his Turkish Bath and *dolce far niente* at "Miller's Hotel," in town, to keeping a livery stable and an Irish boarding-house in Newport, as it took ten horses and as many servants to run the establishment. "There is no accounting for tastes." Mrs Train's father, Col. G. T. M. Davis, has a bijou cottage adjoining his daughter's. The only "celebrity" I have seen here worth noticing is James Gordon Bennett, of the New York *Herald*, who, instead of splurging with a swell four-in-hand, drives a modest one-horse turn-out, but English perfect in all its appointments. When I reflect on what this young journalist has done for Livingstone, for the poor of New York, for Arctic explorations, and, again, for his new African Expedition, and, most of all, the higher tone and broader enterprise he has given the New York *Herald*, there are few men in either hemisphere who command higher praise or a more cosmopolitan admiration.

THE DRAMA.

THE American drama, if such a thing exists, does not appear to have made much progress during the last decade, either in respect to plays or actors. Since Forrest, no "great American tragedian" has arisen to "drown the stage in tears," and to fill the world with the fame of his name. As for actors and actresses, "native and to the manor born," who can name one that deserves to be called "great," or who has won a cosmopolitan reputation? Jefferson is a perfect artist, one may even say genius, in his peculiar line, and that line is limited to almost a single *rôle*. But Jefferson, we believe, was born in England; at all events of English parents. Owen is a capital comedian, but not a newly-risen star. He may in truth be called a veteran, whose glory culminated a quarter of a century ago; but still it may not yet be said of him, "superfluous lags the veteran on the stage." And yet, with a million of honestly-won dollars for his fortune, Owen might retire with grace and comfort, and with no detriment to his reputation. Matilda Heron, of "Camille" fame, has too long been "sick to doomsday with eclipse." Domestic troubles cruelly crushed the lamp of life, but the fire of her genius kept on burning. She is now reconstructing at Miller's Turkish Bath Hotel, and promises soon to re-appear in all her original splendour. With the single exception of "Meg Merrilees" Cushman, America has never produced so great a theatrical genius as Matilda Heron. And she, like "Our Charlotte," shone pre-eminent only in a single *rôle*. We hence conclude that life is too short for perfection in more than one "part," either on the mimic or the real stage. The greatest theatrical production in America to-day is the little "Bijou Heron," a truly legitimate one, the child of Matilda, born of Love and Sorrow. This supernatural *artiste* of ten years has made a *furore* on the stage, and fills the eyes and hearts of all who behold her with "special wonder." Matilda, in her wild way, declares the child has no father but God, and she certainly seems filled with the divine *afflatus*. This little baby-woman, for she is a rare compound of grace and wisdom, simplicity and dignity, innocence and intelligence, has been my *vis-à-vis* several times at dinner, and her beauty does not, like Wordsworth's "Lucy," "make me glad," but *sad*. Truly,

> "A lovely apparition, sent
> To be a moment's ornament."

Bijou Heron would make a great sensation in London. She is altogether the most remarkable phenomenon, the most attractive star, in America. The heartless husband and father, in abandoning his wife and little one for a yellow-haired ballet-girl, like the base Judean,

> "Threw a pearl away
> Richer than all his tribe."

I have heard much of Clara Morris, but did not see her. Her photograph indicates tragic fire. Lester Wallack is the same well-dressed, self-conscious, level actor as of old. Successful management, yachting, trotting, and high-living have not intensified his personation of "High Art." If poets must "learn in suffering what they teach in song," so the dramatic artist must *experience* the emotions he attempts to portray, else all is but "sounding brass and a tinkling cymbal." On Monday evening last there was a notable attempt to inaugurate a genuine American drama, although the play was written by an Englishman, or a Frenchman, for Boucicault's origin, like that of all great geniuses, is somewhat mythical. It was the opening night at Booth's Theatre, and "Belle Lamar," a drama founded on incidents of the late Civil War, was the title of the piece. There was an overflowing house; every inch of standing room being occupied, with the thermometer somewhere in the nineties. For several days the newspapers had piqued public curiosity with the rare dramatic sensation prepared for them by the greatest of living dramatists. So far as the crowd, the applause, and the next day's criticisms go, the play was a great success. It was admirably mounted, and the leading parts were well acted; but I shall venture to call it a failure nevertheless. The events reproduced in the play have not yet ripened into history, and it was positively painful to see the heroic Stonewall Jackson, whose "body is still green in earth," caricatured by a stick of an actor. "Belle Lamar," whose sad career is not unlike that of poor Belle Boyd, will be more acceptable as a play half a century hence, when the late unpleasantness between the North and the South has melted away in the calm, dim haze of history. On board the *Britannic,* "bound for Liverpool," we had, among many other pleasant passengers, Mr Sothern and his two sons, *en route* for Edinburgh. Mr Sothern is altogether the most remarkable and the most successful actor of this or any other age. Since I had the pleasure of "assisting" at his first performance of "Lord Dundreary," at Laura Keene's theatre in New York, some sixteen years ago, he has played this part over four thousand times, for which alone he has received about *one million and a quarter of dollars*. In all the history of the drama there is no record of a success like this. On the 10th of October, after an absence of nearly three years, Mr Sothern will re-appear at the Haymarket as " Lord Dundreary " in " Our American Cousin," but with scarcely a single line of the original part. Mr Sothern will be supported by a charming Australian, Minnie Walton, new to the metropolitan stage. A few words touching my return voyage will close these locomotive observations, although matters of a more didactic nature may follow. The new White Star steamer *Britannic* is a splendid vessel; but if I were going to cross to-morrow, and the *Baltic* and *Britannic* were to start at the same hour I should take the former. It is true the newer ship has some important improvements, as every newest ship ought to have. The *Britannic* has an electric bell attached to every berth, and revolving chairs at the dining tables, with several other little conveniences which her elder sister has not. It also has a pleasant, gentle-voiced Bell for stewardess, pronounced a jewel by the ladies; and yet, and yet—well, we prefer the Baltic. The sea was smooth, the skies were clear, the passengers were jolly, and we reached our old home at the Langham Hotel on the evening of the tenth day. Among the hundred first-class passengers there were half-a-dozen bridal couples, some of them tied for life, or until death or divorce parts them, on the very morning of our departure. The billing and cooing of these love-sick couples made several passengers *see*-sick. One pair in particular were so desperately loving as to feed each other, on deck, with the same spoon, a honeymoon habit, which, we suppose, must have been the origin of "spooning." Another couple incurred the indignation of all on board by utterly neglecting a charming little four-year old boy, who was left to run all over the ship, and whom we named " Charley Ross," thinking he might be the stolen child of Philadelphia. The father of this darling little boy, who became everybody's pet, and my own favourite companion, married a second wife just before leaving New York, and the newly-spliced pair were so deeply involved in their new happiness, so closely locked in each other's arms, that this poor little son, and stepson, was left entirely to the care of the passengers and stewards. "Oh, that this dear little boy's mother could see how her child is neglected," said a kind-hearted Ohio lady. "Thank Heaven she cannot," was my reply. On arriving at the Bar in the Mersey, when the passengers were scrambling on board the "Tug," I took the little fellow along with me, and his "natural protectors " did not seem to discover him until he was landed with the luggage at the Company's wharf in Liverpool. Why did they not ticket him through and send him below? I cannot quit the good ship without a good word for the officers and servants, who spare no efforts to promote the comfort and entertainment of passengers. Other pens will praise the table, and with good reason. Let me thank the Company for the well-selected library. It only lacks the ten bound volumes of the *Cosmopolitan*, which I propose to present to them. With no disrespect to my fellow-passengers, among whom were some very charming and intelligent persons, I found the society of Hood, Jerrold, Thackeray, and Dickens still more agreeable; and when these classics were all read, and re-read, I found a very pleasant companion in "The Anecdotes of Public Men," by my old friend and *confrere* Col. J. W. Forney, whose reminiscences of the past twenty-five years are exceedingly pleasant reading. Col. Forney has for thirty years been one of the leading journalists and politicians of America, besides having occupied for eight years the important post of Secretary of the Senate at Washington. Few writers have had so large and familiar an acquaintance with the leading public men of the United States as the editor of the Philadelphia *Press*. Col. Forney is now in Europe, for the purpose of waking up the Powers and the People to the grand event of the century, the "Centennial of 1876." We venture to predict that he will be the next United States Senator from Pennsylvania. Forney's volume of "Anecdotes" is worthy of a place in European libraries. It is already in the *Cosmopolitan's*.

COSMOPOLITAN MISCELLANIES.

ENGLAND AND THE UNITED STATES.

"WHICH country do you prefer to live in, England or America?" This was the first and last question asked by all classes of people during our recent visit to the United States. After thirteen years abroad, more than two-thirds of the time spent in London, it was naturally supposed that a comparative answer would be easy to give. On the contrary, it is a difficult question to decide, and still more difficult to give satisfactory reasons for the decision. The man who has emigrated to California or Utah, and made a "big pile," comes back with glowing descriptions of the beauty, the salubrity, and the richness of the country; while the unfortunate adventurer who, having toiled and "prospected" in vain for years, returns in poverty and sickness to the home of his childhood to die, gives a very different picture of "life out West." The place we like the best is that in which we have been the happiest—that is, the most successful in receiving all those "good things of this world," which constitute the sum total of the "blessings of life." Exceptional Americans, who, like Peabody, Sturgis, Morgan, and a few others, have easily and rapidly acquired large fortunes in England, are, naturally enough, in love with the land of their adoption; while ninety-nine out of every hundred Americans, fighting for a living on this side of the Atlantic, remain abroad by stress of necessity. From neither of these "types" of the Anglo-American should we look for a just comparison of the intrinsic merits of the two countries. The successful American sees everything *couleur de rose;* the unsuccessful, *tout au contraire.* And so with Englishmen. John Bull praises and curses America according to the results of his investments. Capitalists who have lost money by American railway and mining companies, and by defaulting States, are loud and liberal in their denunciations of the American Republic and American "honour." On the other hand, we now and then come across some lucky Englishman who has doubled his income by American "speculations," and who is profuse in his laudations of the people, the country, and the institutions on the other side of the Atlantic. When the opinions, the judgments, and the feelings of men are governed by the mere caprice of fortune, they are hardly worth quoting. That reverend and sarcastic wag, Sidney Smith, having dabbled in Pennsylvania stocks, which did not pay so well as he hoped, could never do justice to the citizens of that State, or to any other State of the Union. The victims of Erlanger's Confederate Loan have to-day a very bad opinion of the Confederate cause. There is an American lady now in London, a very rich widow, and a Roman Catholic, courted and fêted by all the Romanist nobility of the United Kingdom, who thinks the English people are the best, the noblest, and the most hospitable in the world. *Naturellement.* But, as we have said, exceptional opinions, based on adventitious circumstances, are of little value. And it is the same with persons as with places. X . . . is lovely to me and hateful to you—and *vice versâ.* The journalist, the publicist, the critic, and the historian should have no prejudices. It is very natural to speak well of the bridges that carry us safely over, and ill of those that bring us to grief. And yet one may do justice to the bridge without either praise or censure. It was no fault of the steamer *Atlantic* that she was wrecked on the rocks of Nova Scotia.

Travellers, who write books, are very silly to allow dirty inns and indigestible food to colour their opinions of the countries they visit. But such is the universal fallibility of man. Many a play has been "damned" by critics who have been seated uncomfortably in a theatre. An engineer, recently sent out to New York to survey a Railway property, took a letter of introduction, in a sealed envelope, to a certain Wall Street magnate, containing these words :—" The Report must be *good*, or there'll be a murder." The engineer was received and fêted *comme un prince*, and the Report *will* be good. To return to the question of the comparative merits and attractions of England and America as countries to live in. We profess to have become completely denationalised, to belong to no country, no party, no sect; only to the planet we live in, and to humanity. One must outgrow all these limitations in order to be thoroughly *cosmopolitan*. Therefore we do not judge of places or peoples by the mode of treatment we receive. A man may possibly fall sick in the healthiest country, and, through misunderstanding, receive ill-treatment at the hands of the best of people. To give a just and intelligent estimate of different nations many things must be taken into consideration. In the first place, the climate and the physical qualities and conditions of the country are of the most vital importance. Then come the laws, the government, the institutions, which constitute the political conditions of a people. So far as personal freedom and civil liberty are concerned, there is little to choose between the Monarchy of England and the Republic of America. Liberty, protected by law, is the great problem of both countries, and in both there is no lack of law or of freedom for the general happiness and welfare. Neither in London nor New York does an honest man find his personal freedom impinged by the force of statute law, although the "law of the land" is as omnipresent as the air. Put your foot in it, and it trips you up; violate it, and you are in chains and slavery. The common laws of the two countries are mainly the same. America derived her laws from England; England from Judea; and Judea from the first principles of human nature, the fundamental laws of property and self-preservation, including matrimony, which is but a refined version of property law, although conferring superior rights on the stronger party. This, of course, is owing to the fact that the stronger party established the code; and this is the special grievance of "women's rights" women. The jurisprudence of England and the United States being almost identical, we come to the autonomy of the older and the younger nations. One is a

L

Monarchy, the other a Republic, both essentially democratic, and both having peculiar merits and defects to balance against each other. "Give us an angel from heaven and despotism," said Tom Hood. England, in the person of her good Queen Victoria, has an approach to the "angel," but lacks the benevolent despotism to inaugurate the angelic era. By granting a liberal though a conditional franchise to the masses, the Government of England is essentially a popular Government; that is, a government by the people—in theory at least. Hereditary sovereignty is one of the best features of the British Constitution, while the hereditary Senate is its very worst. The chances are that a "Ruler," born and educated to the Throne, will be a far more graceful and respectable figure-head for the nation than one elected every four years by the capricious choice of universal suffrage, including niggers, chimpanzees, and ignorant "white trash." But a born Senate, like the British House of Lords, is an abomination, an insult to the common sense of civilisation. In the United States, the frequently recurring re-election of President is the greatest of all political evils. Better elect for ten years, or, indeed, for life, and prohibit re-election by an amendment of the Constitution. Unpaid legislation, as in England, might also be adopted in America with salutary results. Law-makers should be men of economy, of thrift, and of pecuniary independence. Solons of the lapstone or goose, who "run for Congress" for the loaves and fishes, had better "stick to their lasts," and allow men of education and of wealth, who have an interest in the State, to serve as "lawgivers" *pro bono publico*. Weighing the two political Constitutions of the old Monarchy and the young Republic in the impartial scales of justice, we leave to each individual reader to declare his own preference. One of the greatest attractions in the United States to free-minded, liberty-loving men is the absolute freedom the people enjoy in regard to "matters of conscience" or religion. There is not only no Established Church in America, but the Federal Constitution recognises no God. As no two minds have the same idea of God, this non-recognition of any particular God-Phantom leaves the intellect of the nation gloriously free from crippling creeds and theological dogmas. At the same time it does not make the people ostensibly irreligious. While they do not bow to the aristocratic God of England, to the more amiable Deity of France, or to the semi-savage Jehovah of the Jews, they quite as generally, and perhaps as devotedly, worship the "unseen and eternal Spirit" as any other people on earth. Indeed, such is the fanaticism of the popular faith, that they boast of having invested *seven hundred millions of dollars* in churches and religious institutions of all denominations, sects, and creeds— including the sterile "Shakers" and the prolific "Mormons"—that priestcraft has ever invented for the subjugation and slavery of the people. This magnificent investment, mostly "in Houses of God" and "parsonages," is almost equal to the amount spent by American ladies during the last five years in silks and diamonds. What a blessed number of bath-houses, soup-houses, and school-houses these millions would have established! But then the great army of priests would have been as ill-fed, as poorly-clothed, and as utterly houseless as Christ Himself. And, pray, what were the people made for but to support priests, soldiers, and the "liberal professions!" The comparative intelligence, refinement, and morality of the two countries is rather a delicate subject of discussion. We purpose to skip it with the safe remark, often repeated in these columns, that London contains the best and the worst of everything to be found in any city on the globe. This applies to men, women, and things, including horses, asses, flowers, fruit, and vegetables. America has more land, brighter skies, and a broader "area of freedom," but no more freedom, except on the Church question, than England.

It is altogether an error to say that in the old country society has been forming, progressing, and refining for a thousand years, while in the new country everything is young, crude, and unsettled. America is simply an *extension of England*. All the elements of English social and political life were carried to New England in the *Mayflower*, and that, too, by the very flower of English civilisation. The "Pilgrim Fathers" were the best-educated men of the epoch, most of whom, forty-one adults, kept their diaries in Latin, as the records of the "Old Colony Society" in Plymouth bear evidence. Nor can we forget the highly-educated followers of Penn, the founder of the State that bears his name, the noble Calvert of Maryland, Fairfax of Virginia, or the accomplished Cavaliers of Carolina and Georgia. In many respects New England sloughed off the hide-bound creeds and impediments of Old England, and the brave citizens of the wilderness rose to a newer, purer, and freer civilisation. The grand idea of a Church without a bishop and a State without a king, gave a new dignity to manhood, and a new inspiration to ambition. Then came the long struggle for independence, which made every man a patriot and every soldier a hero. The "days that tried men's souls" left the young Republic a pure and simple people.

Although sadly degenerated by time, prosperity, and the "admixture of all nations," yet America still retains a full average of national energy and honour; and so far as mere material wealth is concerned, the United States is, beyond all question, the richest nation in the world. With a population of 40,000,000, and more rapidly increasing than any other country, with every variety of climate, soil, and production, it passes the imagination of man to limit its future wealth and power. Therefore, to the young and enterprising, of both sexes and of all classes, who would woo the angel of prosperity in the Future, we say there is no "land of promise" like the land beyond the sea—the land of the free and boundless West, where there is bread, and work, and wealth for all—

"And the sun shines always there."

As for hospitality as a national characteristic, Canon Kingsley will endorse the assertion that the Americans treat their visitors better, *and oftener*, than any other people.

IF IT PLEASES THEM.

A GREAT many English persons and papers are very much exercised by the Pilgrimage to Pontigny, in France. Some five hundred Roman Catholic subjects of Her Most Protestant Majesty Queen Victoria, including such aristocratic names as Lord Edmund Howard, Lord Gainsborough, Lord Archibald Douglas, the Hon. Mrs Douglas, the Hon. Miss Petrie, Mr Petrie, Miss Hope Johnstone, &c., under the lead of Archbishop Manning, have been doing the penance of sea-sickness, and visiting the tomb of St Edmund, who was Archbishop of Canterbury in the thirteenth century. This ancient priest was canonised by the Pope, and is therefore called a " Saint." It is represented to the ignorant and superstitious that St Edmund's holy corpse has not decayed, but is miraculously preserved, and they profess to believe it! Can such intelligent men as Manning, Howard, and Douglas pretend to believe in such monstrous nonsense? *The Cosmopolitan*, with the profoundest reverence for Nature and Truth, but with no respect for priestcraft, will bet all Lombard Street to a picayune that the remains of St Edmund, like those of any other mortal organism six hundred years dead, are undistinguishable dust. The laws of Nature are never suspended or abrogated even for the "benefit of the clergy." The only real objection to these "Pilgrimages" on "boiled peas" is, that they promulgate falsehood in order to prop a rotten system of religion. The priests, knowingly and wickedly, tell the people lies. But this has been their *rôle* from the beginning, and will continue to be, perhaps, for another century or two to come. As for the saintship of Archbishop Edmund, who claims merit for having worn a horse-hair shirt, perhaps over a silk one, are there not men living to-day lives as holy as he? We know a man who has never defiled his body with wine, tobacco, or alcohol, and who lives purely, on cereals, vegetables, and fruits; a man who has never shed blood, nor wronged or ruined a woman, nor told a lie. Why not make pious pilgrimages to the home of this *living* Saint, worth a thousand dead ones, and touch the hem of his garment in pious homage to his chastity and "holiness?" Must a man lie in the earth six hundred years before his virtues are recognised and honoured? But let these Pilgrims go to France, if it pleases them, and draw inspiration from the dead dust of a half-mythical priest, instead of sitting at the feet of living teachers, whose words of wisdom and truth are so hard to hear and obey. It benefits the Railway Companies, and brings grist to Cooke's Excursion Mill. Besides, a little sea-sickness does no harm to over-loaded stomachs, and pious people are even more pious when less bilious. And may not these five hundred devout pilgrims to the shrine of holy dust in unholy France, return to their homes enveloped with an " odour of sanctity " that will sweeten, enrich, and sanctify the murky and ungodly atmosphere of all England? So may it be.

THE POLICY OF INSURANCE.

It is beginning to be a serious question with philosophical economists whether the inestimable sums of money invested in Life, Fire, and Marine Insurance, also in Savings Banks, might not be better employed. We should like to have some clever hand at figures, some expert actuary, to give us the sum total, not only of the amount of capital held by these Companies in the United Kingdom and the United States, but also the annual amounts paid for conducting them, under the head of rents, salaries, and commissions. Nothing impressed us more during a recent visit to the cities of New York, Boston, and Providence, than the multitudinous "palaces" dedicated to Banking, Railway, and Insurance business, and more especially to the latter. The lower part of Broadway is little else than a double row of Insurance buildings, each containing numerous offices, each office filled with a large staff of clerks. And all these Companies pay their presidents, directors, managers, and book-keepers enormous salaries. We hear of hundreds of these officials who receive from 5000 dollars to 20,000 dollars a year. Where does all the money come from to support these costly and magnificent establishments? Out of the insured, of course. The question arises—Would it not be better for the commonwealth if every man was his own insurer and his own savings bank? We are not yet prepared to answer this question of vital interest, and it would take volumes to exhaust the arguments *pro* and *con*. We can only hint at one or two. Insurance offers a premium to crime and dishonesty. Mr Plimsoll has demonstrated beyond all doubt the damning fact that thousands of unseaworthy ships, over-insured, are sent to sea for the purpose of being lost, as a pecuniary speculation, while Fire Insurance records abundantly show that about one-half the fires on insured property are the result of deliberate and diabolic incendiarism. Worse than this, many murders have been committed both by men and women, and that, too, by near relatives, inspired by the hellish thirst of gold to be obtained on Life Insurance policies. "Where will you go when I am dead?" said an anxious dying husband to the wife of his bosom. "Go! why to the Life Insurance Office, of course!" was the cool reply.

A man who has pinched and saved to pay his premium on a £1000 policy for fifty years, certainly deserves credit for providing for his heirs, although they may neither need the money nor thank him for his loving providence. But suppose a sudden blow of adversity compels him to omit the fiftieth payment, and his policy lapses. His heirs get nothing, and all his life-long savings have gone to pay Insurance salaries and to enrich Insurance shareholders. It is this consideration that is turning the attention of thinking men to the general subject of Insurance economy. In the case we have just supposed, a cautious, prudent, thrifty man might have made out of the money invested in his policy ten times the amount insured. Again, he might have speculated unfortunately and lost it all. There is much to be said on both sides of this great question, and we invite a full discussion of the subject in the columns of *The Cosmopolitan*. Meantime the public cannot be too cautious of the character of the Companies to which they trust their sacred savings for *post-mortem* purposes. Rotten Insurance Companies and *bogus* Savings Banks exist in all countries, and the managers of these frauds are criminals of the blackest dye.

AMERICAN PRESS SCANDALS.

TRULY we have fallen upon an age of Iconoclasm. "Rien n'est sacré pour un sapeur," and the "sapeurs" of the Church are everywhere at work. And not only is the Church being insidiously undermined, but reverence for the State, for the "divinity that doth hedge a King" no longer exists. Even the good and gracious Queen Victoria, the model Mother of England, does not escape the slings and arrows of outrageous criticism. We have before us a copy of the New York *Times*, containing a letter from its London correspondent, giving an account of the Royal Servants' Ball at Balmoral, where Her Majesty is depicted, not only as romping in a dance with her grandchildren—all very proper—but as rollicking in a reel with John Brown, "her favourite gillie," which is positively shocking! The correspondent adds, that this unseemly exhibition of Her Majesty is making a great talk in London. The *Times* is owned by a company—that is, by a corporation, with "no soul"—and edited by an imported anti-American Englishman. This is a standing marvel to the American people, as the *Times* assumes to be the leader of the Republican party, and the "organ" of the Grant Administration. Our English readers may get a tolerably just idea of the awkwardness of the situation by "supposing" the *Standard*, the organ of the Disraeli Administration, to be edited by a freshly-imported Yankee. One of the main objects of the *Times* seems to be to convince the public that the *Tribune* is falling off in circulation. The editor is continually proposing to bet that he knows more about his neighbours' business than they themselves know. This may be deemed "honourable competition" by the *Times*' concern, but it is decidedly *un*-English. Whether the *Tribune* prints less or more copies since the loss of Greeley, its immortal founder, it has certainly greatly improved in character by its noble emancipation from the Procrustean bonds and bandages of partisanship. Like the *Herald*—the greatest *news*-paper in the world—the course of the *Tribune* is now as free and refreshing as the river that "windeth at its own sweet will." And no paper that is not free is worth buying or reading. Party newspapers are filled with personal puffs and political tirades, unjust to their objects and insulting to the intelligence of the reader.

Praise and abuse of public men, by a partisan press, is simply a question of politics. And the sectarian criticisms of the so-called "Religious Press," are equally indiscriminate and unjust. "Orthodoxy is my doxy, and your doxy is heterodoxy," sums up the whole philosophy of sectarian intolerance, which forces upon us the sad conclusion that Christianity, instead of uniting the great Family of Man, divides it into hundreds of hostile camps and fierce antagonisms. The only remedy for these universal and obstructive differences is the harmonising influence and all-embracing philosophy of cosmopolitanism. As a sample of the more generous sentiments of the American press, we find the following tribute to the "Powers that be," in a leading article of the New York *Herald*:—" Queen Victoria yesterday commenced the thirty-seventh year of her reign. The day was celebrated in England by the ringing of bells, the firing of salutes, and other demonstrations suitable to the occasion. It is noteworthy that on Tuesday of last week the Pope completed the twenty-seventh year of his reign. It is not unfair, we think, to say that, of all the European rulers of the time, these two are the most popular. They have ruled during the most momentous years of modern history, and we believe we express the general sentiments of the

American people when we say that the death of
the one or the other would be felt to be a world-
wide calamity. In troublous times the Queen has
maintained the dignity of the Throne and won the
love of her subjects. In times of serious peril the
Pope has maintained the authority of the chair of
St Peter, and, if the temporal power is gone, the
spiritual power is greater than ever. Both have
ruled wisely and well, and both have won the
respect of the world." Except among that unhappy
class who cherish a chronic hatred for all their
superiors in character, intellect, wealth, and
station, there is no unkind feeling in America
towards the Queen or the people of England. On
the contrary, there is no city in the world where
the Queen, or any member of the Royal Family,
would received so cordial a welcome as in New
York. And as for " Old England," the blessed
mother of us all, the Americans unanimously
regard it as the greatest country in the world—
except their own.

INTERNATIONAL INHUMANITY.

WE have good reasons for believing that the American Centennial of 1876 will be honoured by the presence of a representative Prince from each of the reigning dynasties of Europe—the Prince of Wales, or one of his Royal brothers, from England; the Prince Imperial of France; the Prince of the Austrias, from Spain; Prince Humbert or Amadeus, from Italy; Prince Frederick, from Germany; and Grand Dukes from Russia, Austria, and other reigning Powers. Will not this great national solemnity be also a fit occasion for convening a "Congress of Nations" in the interest of peace and humanity? It is high time that a world calling itself civilised, to say nothing of the boast of being "Christianised," "evangelised," "redeemed," &c., should stay the hand of human slaughter, stop cutting each other's throats, abolish its gun manufactories, "beat its swords into ploughshares, its spears into pruning-hooks, and learn the art of war no more." So long as

men of the uppermost classes, called " officers,"
deem it an honour to walk the streets with human-
butcher knives dangling at their sides, society
cannot honestly pretend to anything but a state
of semi-barbarism. The colossal fortunes of the
age we live in are made, not by manufacturing
trinkets for Diana of the Ephesians, but by imple-
ments of death for the bloody Moloch of War.
Is not this damnable fact infinitely disgraceful to
our so-called civilisation? And who are responsible for this infamous state of things—the rulers
of the people, the men who make the laws, or
the men who make the law-makers? Human
nature is vicious and perverse, say the Powers
at the head of nations. The people must be
coerced into duty and justice, and that violently,
by bullet and bayonet. Even religious opinions
and dogmas must be maintained and propagated
at the point of the sword, and millions of innocent men must "bite the dust" to keep a King
on his throne or a Pope in his chair. Such is
the record of history, the fallacy of tradition.
And the whole theory and practice of government is a fraud and a lie. Individuals, as a
rule, settle their disputes without coming to
blows, much less to murder, and it would be
vastly easier for nations to arrange their affairs
reasonably and amicably than for individuals, as the
passion involved in the controversy loses its intens-

ity and bitterness in proportion to the numbers that divide and share it. Why, then, is not the Carlist Rebellion in Spain, and the war for Independence in Cuba, summarily settled by the intervention of nations, and an end put to this daily slaughter? Simply because certain powerful and devilish parties have a direct interest in continuing the destructive strife. Gun-makers, powder-makers, and cartridge-makers are all enriched by these wars; while, in Spain, the Priesthood—an institution that professes to represent the " Prince of Peace," and to preach a religion that condemns the shedding of human blood as the greatest of all crimes—is the very source and soul of the Rebellion. And yet the neighbouring Powers look on the bloody carnage with their hands in their pockets! Yes, literally, with their hands in their pockets, clinking the guineas coined from the blood of the people—the victims of sectarian and political ambition! Prince Alfonso, by the law of Spain, is the rightful heir to the Throne. If Spain has not the power to place him there, let the nations, in the name of Humanity, jointly come to her assistance. If the people of Spain, after a full and fair *plébiscite*, do not wish their young Prince to reign over them as Alfonso XI., then let them choose whom they will. And so of France, although so long as the Provisional Government of M'Mahon is able to " keep the peace," the question of Restoration is not so urgent as in

Spain. As for poor Cuba, the United States alone is responsible for the long suffering of the "patriots" in their brave and desperate struggle for liberty. But this charge against the United States is altogether too vague, and does great injustice to the American people. We shall narrow it down, and bring it directly home to the Government at Washington. Still closer, and more pointedly, we charge the Secretary of State, Hamilton Fish, as solely responsible for the disastrous continuance of this six years' war in the island of Cuba. Mr Fish alone has stood between that patriotic band and Cuban Independence. President Grant is for intervention, the whole American people are for intervention, but Prime Minister Fish is permitted by an "unscrupulous Providence" to restrain, through the omnipotence of an iron-clad statute, the sympathetic impulses of 40,000,000 of people! "There is not water enough in all great Neptune's ocean to wash this blood clean from *his* hands." Let us have a Peace and Humanity Congress at Philadelphia—the Beautiful City of Brotherly Love—in 1876, and put an end to this brutal war trade and international inhumanity. Let the murder-munition men howl till Hell echoes. There will be a new anthem of joy heard in the Heavens in glad response to this Centennial Song of Peace.

ROMANISM AND MASONRY.

ROME rejoices. Lord Ripon, with his £60,000 a year, has joined the Catholic Church, and His Holiness the Pope is about to present the noble "pervert" with a sacred souvenir. The Prince of Wales succeeds his late "Grand Superior" as Head-Centre of British Freemasonry. These "changes" are regarded by the public generally, and by the *Times* particularly, as very important events, big with the fate of men and empires. Cosmopolitanism, which has passed all sectarian limits, all political stations, all social organisations, looks upon these "great events" as the merest trifles, the falling of a leaf, the evolution of a cloud, the apparition of a vapour. Lord Ripon has gone over to Rome, and the sun continues to rise and set. Lord Ripon is an apostate from the Church of his fathers, the Established Church of England; and the rivers still flow on to the sea. Lord Ripon accepts the dogma of Immaculate Conception and human infallibility, and Mother Nature inexorably fulfils the great law of her existence, as it was in the beginning, is now, and shall be for evermore! The difference between Ritualism and Romanism is the difference between mock turtle and real turtle. Some prefer to swallow the genuine article, without questioning; others, the simulated preparation, with more or less of hesitation and doubt. In joining the Roman Church, a man surrenders his reason, and blindly gulps the "Syllabus." To be a "good Catholic," there must be no more free thinking, no more logic, no more philosophy. All that is required is the old "fides Carbonaria"—that is, to believe what the Church believes, no matter how preposterous, how monstrous the creed may be. The Church assumes to be wiser than science, greater than Nature, and less fallible than the motions and the mathematics of the solar system. The Protestant Church, while professing to reject these tyrannous assumptions of the Roman Hierarchy, and reserving to itself the inalienable birthright of reason and freedom, fails to embody, either in faith or practice, the very first principles it professes. Protestantism, as represented by the Established Church of England, is neither liberal, logical, nor tolerant. Both Churches have made of Christianity a religion of mysticism and mythology, and the "members" of both sects are mainly hypocrites, although the great majority, it is charity to believe, have not the intelligence to know it. In the first place, we insist that no intelligent, educated mind of the present century really believes in the miraculous absurdities which the Roman Church, the English Church, or any other Church, teach and preach as doctrines "essential to salvation." They all pretend to believe that the Author of Christianity was supernaturally begotten, and that the Palestine peasant girl who gave him birth is the veritable Mother of God! The statement of this impossible dogma is sufficient for its refutation. But it is no use to argue with men who assert that water runs uphill, or that the sun revolves round the earth. The great practical error of all the Churches, and of all Religions, is, that they profess to save men *after* they are dead, and not to make them good and happy while living. What mean all these costly "Houses of God," all these funeral prayers and burning candles? Is it to comfort and benefit the living? Not at all. It is the *future* salvation of miserable sinners that the Church is always looking after, not the present welfare of sick and suffering humanity. In ninety-nine cases out of every hundred, if men could be made comfortable for this life, they would willingly "jump the life to come." When the saints come together weekly to pray that poor men's souls may be kept out of Hell throughout Eternity, let them interpolate in their "petitions" an earnest wish that these "perishing sinners" may find the bread of life to-day and means to pay their rent. Furthermore, they might prove their sincerity, and add efficacy to their prayers, by taking up contributions for this very purpose, instead of carrying round the hat for the "poor heathen abroad," which means for the salaries of Foreign Missionary Societies. Practical charity is what poor sinners are dying for, not for lack of prayers and precepts. To help a suffering fellow-man through the real troubles of to-day is a thousand times better than praying that he may escape some doubtful danger to-morrow. A man dying of starvation will gladly accept a loaf of life-saving bread instead of prayers for his soul's repose after death. This is a world of realities, not illusions. We know what we are, and what we want to-day; we know not where we shall be, or what we may need, to-morrow. In fact, we positively know absolutely nothing beyond the grave. It is the present life, not the future, that concerns us most. If the Churches of all sects and creeds would take this practical, *cosmopolitan* view of their duties, there would be a Religion of Humanity far above all these petty and petulant ecclesiastical divisions of Rome, and Greece, and England. The world would then consist of but one harmonious Family of Nations, with one Church and one State at the head of all. The ostracism of the secret society of Freemasons by the Roman Church is characteristic of the intolerance of that ancient, moss-grown, worm-eaten, ivy-bound Hierarchy. It is the policy of the Church to allow its members the possession of no secrets, especially its female members. The Confessional must know all. If a woman has "sinned," she must unbosom the delicate secret to her " Father Confessor," who, of course, administers ghostly admonition, at the same time assuring the fair penitent that, having discovered a worm in the fruit, there is no harm in taking a bite himself. The Roman Priests manage these "pastoral relations" and " nest-hiding" scenes much better than bungling Protestants—Beecher, for instance, over whose imprudent tilt on Elizabeth more noise is made than at any similar *chute* since the " Fall of Adam." But the Rev. Beecher is only following in the footsteps of the Saints of Old, whom he and all his craft are constantly holding up to admiring congregations as models worthy of all imitation. Abraham, Isaac, and Jacob, Moses,

David and Solomon, were all, according to the "Sacred Word," more or less guilty of Brigham Youngamy. And Beecher is probably neither better nor worse than his "holy examples." As for the great battle between the Old Catholics and the Reformers, it is growing hotter and hotter, and promises to be the great event of the close of the century. The Masons, and all Secret Societies, will now take active part against Mother Church, and when Pio Nono closes his eyes, there will be an earthquake in the Vatican. In the meantime it may be interesting to refer to a letter from the Pope—addressed to the Archbishop of Paris—on the subject of Masonry some years ago. In this letter all Secret Societies are denounced as "sects of impiety, bound only by complicity in odious crimes, full of perverse manœuvres and diabolical crimes; corrupters of morals, and destroyers of every idea of honour, truth, and justice; propagators of monstrous opinions; disseminators of abominable vices and unheard-of wickedness, and capable, if possible, of driving God from Heaven." This is pretty strong. It should, however, be remembered that it is admitted by Masonic writers that not the Papacy, but the States-General of Holland, had the discredit of beginning the persecutions of Masons. Not until 1738 did Clement XII. fulminate his bull against Masonry.

Freemason writers are fond of asserting that the present Pope himself once belonged to the fraternity. And when by his orders the priests of Madrid refused to perform the services of the Church over the body of Prince Henry of Bourbon, they accused him of violation of his Masonic oath, and they asserted that the statements made in his letter to M. Darboy were either calumnies, or were flagrant infringements of the vow which he took on entering the Order. We close with one word for the priests of all denominations: The man who preaches better things than he practises, whose sermon is holier than his life, is a fraud.

ENGLISH GIRLS IN LONDON.

CERTAIN long-sighted philanthropists have been getting up a sympathy meeting in Manchester in behalf of the "poor English girls in Paris," at which the Bishop of Manchester presided. Are these good people aware of the fact that the City of London swarms with poor English girls, who are in quite as wretched a condition as any of their countrywomen in Paris? It is estimated that a hundred thousand prostitutes nightly hunt for bread in the streets of the Great Metropolis, infesting all its highways and byways. We say, deliberately, hunt for bread, or rather for money, as this is the motive of nine out of every ten of these miserable women who haunt the streets in pursuit of their disreputable vocation. And they belong to all classes and conditions of society, including married, unmarried, and widowed. From Pall Mall to Portland Place, and from twilight to midnight, a countless multitude of these sad beggars lie in wait for their prey. But it is poverty, not passion, that sends these women into the street to traffic with strangers in a way repugnant to every instinct of woman's nature. At first they will importune a man to accompany them home, or offer to go home with him, and, on being refused, will beg piteously for a shilling, a glass of beer, or of gin. No doubt drink is the principal cause of all this misery. Excited by drink, a woman commits her first *faux pas*, and then she goes on drinking to stupefy her sensibilities, and drown her sense of shame. And London is inundated with these miserable sinners. But our philanthropists overlook all this sin and suffering at home, and go over to the gay capital of France to find a field for the exercise of their charities. They want £10,000 to build a " Home " in Paris for English women stranded there. Not less than £1,000,000 is needed here in London to relieve the suffering and starvation of these 100,000 street-walkers, who are struggling to live on the " wages of sin," many of whom dare not enter their rooms at night without their " wages " in their pockets. And yet our goody-goody Church-folk pass by all this misery on their own doorsteps, and hold their " regular prayer-meetings," and "take up contributions " for the conversion of the happy heathen of Borrioboolagha! Aristocratic ladies despise these poor Magdalenes of the streets, and gather up their immaculate robes whenever one of "these women" passes, as if a pestilence approached. At the same time Madame Respectability, assuming a virtue that she does not possess, may be a monster of falsehood, infidelity, and hypocrisy, and a thousand times more guilty in the sight of Infinite Purity than these poor honest prostitutes on whom she casts a withering look of scornful contempt. The judgments of men, and of women too, are sometimes unjust. If we had the purse of a Rothschild or a Coutts, we would not go to Paris or to China for the objects of our charity, but would distribute the "bread of life" freely along Regent Street among the multitude of hungry and unhappy women who nightly haunt that fashionable promenade.

THE MARVELLOUS COUNTRY.

THIS is the attractive title of an exceedingly fascinating book, written by Samuel Woodworth Cozzens, and published by Sampson Low & Co., in a handsome volume of 532 pages, illustrated by over 100 engravings. We have read the work at a single sitting, and with an interest unsurpassed even by the scientific fictions of Jules Verne. The author has passed three years in the " Marvellous Country " of Arizona and New Mexico, and his descriptions, which have the marks of authenticity, are of the most picturesque, romantic, and thrilling character. Mr Cozzens meets and quotes men from whose lips we have often heard of the beautiful scenery, the mountain sublimity, and the mineral marvels which form the subject of his wonderful book. General Gadsden, the American Minister, who negotiated the Mexican Treaty, at whose pleasant plantation in South Carolina we have heard of the inestimable value of the "Gadsden Purchase;" John R. Bartlett, the United States

Commissioner to settle the "Boundary Question" between Mexico and the United States; Sylvester Mowry, one of the earliest American settlers in Arizona, and the first to represent the Territory at Washington; J. Ross Browne, who visited the Mines as United States Surveyor; and Colonel C. D. Poston, also a representative from Arizona at Washington, and who has long lived in that "Marvellous Country" as manager of a great Mining Company; from each and all of these actual "surveyors of the land" we have had the same general report now more fully and graphically given in the charming volume before us. We should like to give our readers a *résumé* of the contents of this rare work; but, better still, if we can only induce them to read it, as the perusal cannot fail to turn the footsteps of European travellers towards the "Marvellous Country," many of whom would doubtless be inclined to remain there for life, or at least long enough to carve their fortunes from the silver mountains of Arizona and Sonora. In 1514, twenty-two years after the discovery of the New World by Columbus, Cortez conquered Mexico, and found the Aztecs, as the people were then called, in possession of immense quantities of gold, silver, and precious stones. Hence the name of *El Dorado* given to the new country by the Spaniards. To the question—"Where did all this treasure come from?"—Montezuma's only reply, even when put to the torture, was, "from the North-West," from a country known as Cibola, the Buffalo, far beyond the limits of Montezuma's empire. The Cibola of that day is the Arizona of this, which means "the silver-bearing land." No wonder that the Mexicans were so reluctant to cede this rich territory to the United States for the comparatively insignificant sum of 10,000,000 of dollars. It is confidently predicted that the product of a single Arizona silver mine will reach 100,000,000 dollars in a single year. In the monastery of Dolores, in Zacatecas, there are parchment records of Father Kino, who, in the year 1658, explored this "Marvellous Country" alone, in the interest of his Church, "the Cross his only protection, the wilderness his only purveyor," and found gold and silver utensils more plentiful than iron. No doubt this brave old monk followed the course of the Santa Cruz river, in what is now the province of Sonora, until he reached its junction with the Gila. Father Kino describes the people as primitive and patriarchal, whose flocks and herds were immense, whose religion was Sun-worship, and upon whose altars a flame of devotion was, and still is, always burning. From that day to this the people have changed but little, and the country still less. There are the wonderful silver mines, as rich and as inexhaustible as in the time of the Montezumas; there is the "Organ Mountain," with its forty various-coloured pipes gleaming in the sun; there are the wonderful cities of natural architecture, rivalling the work of man; the cactus tree, four feet in diameter, fifty feet high, the trunk fluted like a Corinthian column, and bursting into bloom of indescribable splendour at the top; and there are curious mounds, enchanting valleys, fragrant forests, flowing streams, innumerable birds of strange bright plumage, and all the varied products of nature and of civilisation in the way of fruits, vegetables, cereals, &c. The book is rightly named. It is indeed a "Marvellous Country." Mr Cozzens gives us nothing particularly new in regard to the richness of the mines of Arizona and Sonora. We have had all the facts and figures in a more exact form in the official reports of Browne, Bartlett, Pumpelly, and others. The latter author, who deserves to be called the Humboldt of America, in his "Notes of a Five Years' Journey Round the World," is full of most valuable information in regard to Arizona. To the question why these rich mines have been comparatively neglected since the acquisition of the Territory by the United

States, two reasons may be given as sufficient answer :—The Civil War and the Apache Indians. The former is at an end, and the Indians are nearly all exterminated. Cochise, the vindictive and revengeful Chief, is dead, and the remnant of his hostile tribe will soon be utterly extinct. The only way to reform an Apache is to kill him. After reading the horrible details of their cruelties, even a "Quaker Commissioner" would be disposed to change his policy of conciliation for one of extermination. Like beasts and birds of prey, rattlesnakes, and other venomous reptiles, the sooner these pestilential "Injins" are "improved" from the face of the earth the better for themselves and the rest of mankind. To return to the natural wonders of this "Marvellous Country." Forty miles west of the Rio Grande is the river Mimbres, which occasionally sinks and disappears in the plains, re-appearing miles below. This is one of the unique wonders of the world. Then there is the "Ojo Caliente," hot spring, on the top of a mound 962 feet in circumference at the base, and 46 feet in height. The water sustains a perpetual temperature of 135° Fahrenheit, and when cooled is drinkable. For hot bathing it is wonderfully efficacious in all scrofulous complaints. What an attraction for a *grand hôtel des invalides!* In the Mesilla Valley we have the famous El Paso grape, of which a hundred thousand gallons of wine are annually made, equal to the finest Port or Burgundy. The El Paso vine was introduced by the priests from Portugal in the year 1680. Among other marvellous customs of the country we give the following " religious anecdote : "—Our author attends a cock-fight, " after vespers, in the yard of the church, at which silver ounces freely changed hands. Each cock was armed with the old-fashioned Spanish slasher, a long, thin, steel blade, shaped somewhat like a hoop, and most effective in destroying the life of the bird in whose body it is once sheathed. The priest who officiated at vespers was the owner of the winning cock, his opponent having been brought from Tucson. Of course we congratulated him upon his good fortune, and his hearty *mil gracias* convinced us that his soul was quite as much with his bird as it had been with his service." Mr Cozzens gives the following picture of Tubac, where he found " the *élite* of Arizona. It was also the headquarters of the Arizona Mining Company; and it was here that we met Mr Poston, the agent and superintendent of the Company. The town itself was very attractive, with its beautiful groves of acacias, its peach orchards, and its pomegranates, situated, as it is, immediately on the banks of the Santa Cruz, and embowered in the most luxuriant foliage. In close proximity to this town are to be found the Santa Rita, the Heintzleman, and the Cerro Gordo mines, the richest yet discovered in the Territory." Among the Custom-House archives of Guaymas, the seaport of Sonora, is found the "entry," in 1683, of a mass of virgin silver weighing 2800 lbs., which was claimed for the King as a "curiosity." Humboldt says that "up to the beginning of the present century, the quantity of silver taken from these mines has exceeded that of gold in the ratio of 46 to 1." When the Southern Pacific Railroad reaches Tucson, as it is bound to do at no distant date, and a hundred thousand coolies are at work in the Santa Rita Mines, in the lovely Santa Rita Valley, where the thermometer stands at 70° Fahrenheit all the year round, there will be such an influx of the precious metals from that "Marvellous Country" as the world has never seen since the days of Cortez. We have no knowledge of the author of this "marvellous" book, except that he is an American; but we must give him credit for one of the most interesting and valuable works of travel and adventure we have ever read. Neither Humboldt, Ward, Pumpelly, nor any other author has given us so fascinating a panorama of the Silver Land of Arizona, the Treasure-House of the Montezumas, the El Dorado of Cortez, the rich Mission-field of the

Jesuits, the most "Marvellous Country" in that New World which Columbus gave to the Kingdom of Castille and Leon, a new jewel to the Crown of Ferdinand and Isabella.

END OF THE PRETENDER.

THE report of the serious wounding of Don Carlos lacks confirmation. We fear it is not true. This sounds cruel, inhuman; but, considering only the greatest good of the greatest number, the death of this stupid Pretender, the catspaw of the Ultramontanes, would be a public blessing. The life of this arrant traitor is worth no more than that of tens of thousands who have fallen in his foolish cause; besides, the crime of treason long since doomed the Pretender to death. Whether he is now mortally wounded or not, the cause of the Carlists, which was a lost cause from the beginning, must soon collapse in a miserable *fiasco*. It has been kept alive by the Priests, who have squeezed the "sinews of war" from their bigoted and benighted followers. No end of blood and treasure has been sacrificed in this wicked and hopeless Rebellion, which is now approaching the last gasp. Therefore it is not unreasonable nor unjust to desire the instant suppression of a great crime by

the death of the greatest criminal. Carlism has no
sympathy in Europe outside the Roman Church,
and only among those Ultramontanes who abandon
reason, common sense, and every attribute of manhood to obey the dictates of Priestcraft. The war
in Spain is a war between Reason and Superstition,
between Treason and Legitimacy. The Rightful
Heir to the Throne, now a student in England, is
naturally regarded by the better classes of the
Spanish people just as much their future King as
the Prince of Wales is so regarded by the people of
England. In either case, an honest popular *plebi-
scite* would only seat the Rightful Heir more firmly
on the Throne. We repeat, the death of the Pretender and Traitor Carlos, a thick-headed youth
with more ambition than brains, would be an event
for universal rejoicing, especially to the poor country
that has lost by his wicked pretensions so much
blood and treasure.

THE DEVIL'S INVENTION.

It is generally believed that gunpowder was invented by a "Heathen Chinee." We are inclined to doubt the tradition from the fact that the Chinese at that epoch had no guns, and did not use explosives for blasting purposes. Considering the destructiveness of this infernal commodity, we must regard gunpowder as the Devil's own invention. Not that we believe in a personal Devil, but we do believe in the existence of men endowed with all diabolical passions and attributes, which practically amounts to the same thing. The number of deaths caused, and the amount of property destroyed, by the use of this "villainous saltpetre" is altogether beyond our arithmetic to calculate. As for any good that has resulted from the invention we leave others to estimate. And now, in addition to this fearful explosive, science has given us dynamite, glycerine, and gun-cotton, and there is more than enough of these deadly agents in the warehouses of London to blow the entire city to smithereens.

If the shaking up of the Regent's Park explosion opens the eyes of the authorities to the perils to which we are momently exposed, it will prove a blessing in disguise, considering how few lives were lost. Half-a-million sterling may, perhaps, repair the damages of *this* disaster, while a hundred millions would not cover the possible loss of a similar calamity in the heart of the metropolis. As the losses by the late calamity will principally fall on house-owners, no doubt an energetic effort will be made to guard against a repetition of the catastrophe. In the meantime, *somebody* in authority should instantly banish all these dangerous explosives to a safe distance from all human habitations. Parliament is not in session, and, when it meets, red-tape movements are slow. Some time since, we are told, there was a great fire at Bromley Rice Mills, and it was discovered that close under the blazing pile was a barge laden with thirty tons of gunpowder—six times as much as caused the destruction in St John's Wood. The barrels were covered with tarpaulin; several pieces of blazing timber fell from the burning building on this covering, but were plucked away by courageous hands, and thus the cargo and the community were saved. The carriage of gunpowder through London is an event of very frequent occurrence. At Blackwall Stairs alone 132 tons were shipped in 1872, and 122 tons in 1873; other shipments took place at Wapping, Bow Creek, and elsewhere. These shipments are made in quantities varying up to twenty tons, and are conducted quite legally; but Major Majendie, in stating this to the Select Committee, added these significant words :—" It was carried in open carts, which are, in my opinion, quite unsuitable for the conveyance of powder through populous places; also, in putting the powder into barges and taking it out of barges, I am told it is a common thing for the barrels to break and the powder to be spilt, and no special precautions are taken by laying down cloths, proper boats, or otherwise; add to that, that there is no power of interference on the part of the police in the case of people smoking in the neighbourhood. And this is a point to which I wish to call most particular attention." During the American Civil War no less than 500 tons of gunpowder were stored in the harbour of New York. A single spark from a careless smoker would have blown the city to atoms. On the whole, except for "sporting" purposes, gunpowder might as well be abolished. Its measure of mischief is about filled up. Society can exist without this destructive element, and that, too, more happily and more securely. Is there not, among all the numberless worlds of the Solar System, at least one where there are no guns, or swords, or bayonets, nor professional human butchers called soldiers? Such a world would be a very pleasant one to settle in. One would not object to passing through the Dark Valley in order to reach it.

THE DREAMLAND OF THE PACIFIC.

THE untravelled multitude, among all civilised nations, entertain a vague belief in the existence of certain "Islands of the Blest," situated somewhere in the South Pacific Ocean, where peace, plenty, and health are the normal condition of man, making life one long dream, or rather reality of happiness. Such is the romantic land of Melville's "Omoo and Typee," the "Navigators' Islands" of the Dutch, the Samoan group of Wilkes, and our latest editions of "maps of the world." This fair cluster of Polynesians is composed of nine islands lying between 13° 27' and 14° 18' south of the equator, and between 169° 28' and 172° 48' west longitude. They are of volcanic origin, and only as recently as 1866 "a great column of fire burst forth from the ocean, between Manua and Oloosinga, rising like a pillar to the height of a thousand or more feet, and continuing for a period of two weeks." All the mountains of the Samoan Islands are extinct craters;—another argument in favour of the igneous origin of all things mundane—effects of the one great cause—which always lead us reverently back to the omnipotent Sun, the Father of Light, and Life, and Motion. Our attention has been freshly called to these beautiful " Pacific Isles " by an exceedingly interesting Report recently made by Colonel A. B. Steinberger to the Secretary of State at Washington, and communicated to the Senate in a Message from the President on the 21st of April 1874. Colonel Steinberger is a young man of rare ability and promise. When scarcely of age, this brave young pioneer, to protect his little band from a pitiless Rocky Mountain snow-storm, erected the first hut on the site of the flourishing city of Denver. In the early part of 1873 Colonel Steinberger was commissioned by the President to make a survey of the Islands of Samoa, for which duty he embarked from San Francisco in the pilot-boat *Fanny*, a schooner of forty-three tons, on June 29th of the same year. The Report now before us is an exceedingly valuable contribution to the geographical knowledge of the world, and will doubtless make the intelligent and scientific author an honorary member of all the Geographical and Ethnological Societies of Europe and America. The marvels of those comparatively unknown Islands are stranger than the romantic pictures of Dreamland to be gathered from the pages of Richard Dana, Ross Browne, Herman Melville, Dr Mayo, or any of the numerous authors who, skirting these "Islands of the Blest," and scenting their "spicy breezes," have thrown around them the iris-hued tints of Paradise. But truth is always more wonderful, more beautiful, and more sublime than fiction. Our surveyor's plain facts are more fascinating than the poetic fancies of the novelists. In last week's *Cosmopolitan* we wrote, *con amore*, of "The Marvellous Country" of New Mexico, the wonderful Silver Land of Arizona and Sonora, and our little sketch is already re-appearing in the French press. We now call the attention of our readers to another wonder-land of a very different description, inhabited by people of a very different character, far away in the blue Pacific—

> "That softer clime that lies
> In ten degrees of more effulgent skies."

There we find that sacred bird, the veritable "Dodo," inhabiting the most lonely parts of inaccessible mountains, and only eaten by great chiefs. Colonel Steinberger brought home a live specimen, which proved to be the "tooth-billed pigeon," having three teeth upon either side of the lower mandible. And there, too, although snakes are numerous, none are venomous, and one species (*vivimi gata*) crows like a cock! In 1838 Commodore Wilkes visited this charming group of Islands, and all who have read his narrative will remember the lovely little Princess "Emma." Colonel Steinberger found her last year a beautiful woman of fifty. The aggregate population of the group is about 36,000, of whom Upolu has 16,000 and Savaii 12,000. The entire area of these Islands, according to Wilkes, is 1650 square miles. The products embrace almost every kind of fruits and vegetables known in the tropics. The magnificent timber-trees are unsurpassed in size, beauty, and variety. Col. Steinberger brought home forty-one different specimens. The banyan flourishes in all its grandeur and glory. The inhabitants are amiable, meek, and melancholy, of a dark olive complexion, resembling polished copper. The male Samoan is tall, erect, proud in bearing, with smooth, straight, and well-rounded limbs. The females are generally slight, especially the young girls; erect and symmetrical, easy and graceful in their movements, "the charm of light-heartedness seeming to follow every action." Venereal disease is unknown; and maidens have to submit to a test of their virginity before the nuptial knot is tied. With even-handed justice, adultery in both sexes is punished with two years of hard labour on the public roads. Since the year 1830 these innocent and amiable "heathen" have all been converted to Christianity, at first through the preaching of "Jimmy the Sweet," who could neither read nor write, and of "Dan the Convict," who captured the *Roma*, murdered the captain, burnt the ship, and landed in Savaii as a volunteer missionary. It was then that the Rev. John Williams, now known as "the martyr," took up the "Tale of Redemption," and carried it triumphantly through the Islands. Now every child can read and write, repeat the Catechism, and sing hymns as glibly as any Sunday-scholar in Europe. "With them Sunday is a day of rest and religious devotion. Food is collected on Friday and prepared on Saturday. On the Sabbath scarcely a boat is to be seen; the hunter is never in the woods during its sacred hours. Attendance upon church-meetings affords almost the only sign of life; even the sports of the children are sacrificed, in a large degree, to the strict observance of the day. To a stranger, the village seems deserted." The laws recently enacted for the government of these Islands are more "advanced" than those of "the most favoured nations of Europe." The commerce of Samoa is monopolised virtually by Germany, and that by the single mercantile house of Goddefroy & Co., of Hamburg, represented at Apia, the principal port, by Mr Alfred Poppe. During the fifty-five days that Col. Steinberger's schooner was in port, the above firm took away no less than 5230 tons of copra, dried cocoa, worth 95 dollars a ton in Europe, for which they paid the natives about 20 dollars a ton. Col. Steinberger found everywhere the chiefs and the people anxious to come under the protection of the United States, and has so reported to the Powers at Washington. So we may look for the annexation of the Samoan group to the Great Republic at no distant date. If so, we hope that Col. Steinberger will be appointed Governor of these lovely Islands, of which he has given so good a Report. Mr Secretary Fish has shown great sagacity and statesmanship in this Samoan movement. He could not have selected a better Commissioner for the purpose than Col. Steinberger, who is already regarded as *de facto* Chief of the Samoan Islands, as he not only made enthusiastic friends of the natives, but was also warmly welcomed by the missionaries, of whose benevolent labours he speaks in the strongest terms.

AMERICAN BONDS AND ENGLISH CONSOLS.

WHILE the promises to pay of the British Government yield only three per cent. interest per annum, and the United States Bonds pay five per cent., it is simply a mathematical fact that the latter are *forty per cent. better* than the former. With so great a difference in favour of American investments, why does not every holder of English Consols convert them at once into American Bonds? Simply because the high rate of interest implies a doubt in regard to the validity of the security. If the man who holds £10,000 in the English Funds, deriving therefrom an income of £300 a year, had as much confidence in the financial honour and solvency of the American Government as in the English, he would instantly change his investment into American Five per Cent. Bonds, and swell his income to £500 a year, just forty per cent. more than what he is now receiving. The question, then, of the absolute *security* of American "Securities" is one of the utmost importance to all who are living on Consols. It involves many considerations — the form and stability of the Government, the character of the people, and the resources of the country. From the very first issue of the *Cosmopolitan*, soon after the close of the Civil War, we have constantly insisted that the public debt of the United States was "good;" that the interest thereon would be promptly paid in gold; that the Union of the States was assured, at least for the next half century; and that the National Debt, annually diminishing, might easily be totally extinguished before the year 1900. With this firm faith in the stability of American institutions, in the integrity of the American people, and in the infinite resources of American industry, applied to inexhaustible elements of agricultural and mineral wealth, the *Cosmopolitan*, nine years ago, began to urge upon the authorities at Washington the feasibility of reducing the interest on the public debt from seven to five per cent., and even to four. Any one who is curious to verify this fact may refer to the files of the paper in this office, or to the bound volumes of the *Cosmopolitan* in the British Museum. The result of these efforts may be gathered from the fact that the United States

Treasury Department has established an office in London, in the banking-house of the Rothschilds, with John P. Bigelow, Esq., as administrator, for the purpose of exchanging Five per Cent. United States Bonds for those bearing a higher rate of interest, and for selling American Five per Cents. at the rates of premium quoted from day to day in the money markets of Europe. When we estimate the many millions saved to the American taxpayers by this reduction of interest, may not the *Cosmopolitan* justly indulge in the self-complacent feeling of having "done the State some service?" The difference between six per cent. and five per cent. a year on £400,000,000 is £4,000,000, or 20,000,000 of dollars. When the American Chancellor of the Exchequer has reduced all his interest-bearing debt to five per cent., he should lose no time in making another 25 per cent. saving by the issue of Four per Cent. Bonds, which even then would be a 25 per cent. better investment than English Consols. The *Standard*, an ultra-Conservative, and intensely anti-Republican Journal, in a recent article endeavours to frighten capitalists by the magnitude of the American Debt, and what it is pleased to call "democratic extravagance." Taking Mr Blaine's estimate of all the National, State, County, and Municipal obligations, the *Standard* chuckles over the fact that the young Republic of America, not yet a century old, has become as deeply involved in debt as the ancient Monarchy of England, whose "flag has braved a thousand years the battle and the breeze." In reply to this, we will venture the prediction that, long before the Government of the United States is as old as England, it will have no debt at all. In round numbers the Federal debt of America is £428,000,000, of which £12,800,000 has been spent in the construction of the Pacific Railway, and the awful balance in "crushing out the Rebellion." According to Mr Blaine, the aggregate of the State debts amounts to £78,000,000, the County debts to £36,000,000, and the Municipal debts to £114,000,000. "And Mr Blaine deliberately gives it as his opinion"—we are now quoting the *Standard*—"that, so recklessly have the loans been contracted, no town or county has received ten shillings' worth of benefit for each pound raised. But, however that may be, we find, after all the repudiation that has been practised, that the National Debts of the United States still amount to about £508,000,000 sterling, while the local debts reach at least £150,000,000. So much for the economy of democratic Government in less than a century."

The sarcasm is just. We have no disposition and no argument to defend the extravagance or the corruption of the American Government. At the same time, we insist that the spendthrift will pay his debts to the uttermost farthing. Therefore, we have no hesitation in calling the attention of capitalists to the superiority of American Bonds over English Consols as a permanent investment. As a general rule these investments have proved gold mines to Europeans. The Rothschilds bought American securities by the bushel at 40 cents on the dollar, and which now "stand them in" *less than nothing;* while the great bulk of United States Bonds held in Germany have been paid in full by ten years' interest. So that, as a mere matter of figures, if hundreds of millions of these Bonds were repudiated to-day, original holders would not lose a penny by their investment. In regard to the several State debts, there is now a better prospect than ever of their assumption by the Federal Government. Great Britain used to be the most heavily indebted nation of the world; but France, since her late war of 1870–71, comes first, England second, and the United States third. The figures are for the years 1873–74 :—

	Aggregate debt.	Population.	Debt per capita.
France	$4,551,200,000	36,102,921	$126
Great Britain	3,925,000,000	31,857,338	123
United States	2,230,000,000	38,558,371	57

We may measure the burden of public debt by the annual interest which it imposes upon the taxpayers. This is the method of comparison most in vogue on the Continent of Europe, and it is unquestionably a fairer way of estimating it, so far as the current burdens and resources are concerned, than that which looks only at the aggregate amount of the debt. For it must be remembered that the rate per cent. of interest that is paid, varies very widely in different nations and upon different portions of the same nation. While Great Britain pays only three per cent. annual interest on her vast public debt of four thousand millions of dollars, the United States, on the other hand, pays rather more than five per cent. on the larger share of her National Debt. Besides, we must consider, in any estimate of this character, that some national debts (and notably that of Great Britain) are not expected to be paid, but to rest as a permanent charge upon the resources of the country and a method of investment for the capital and savings of all classes. Doubtless a debt which is to be liquidated so as to reduce it to nothing in a certain or uncertain number of years, should be estimated as to its aggregate amount rather than as to its annual charge in the shape of interest. But in regard to a debt which it is never destined to liquidate, but to continue paying interest on for a permanent or indefinite period, the interest charge is the factor of most importance in determining its burden upon the people. A debt of 4,000,000,000 dollars at three per cent. is less burdensome than a debt of 2,500,000,000 dollars would be at five per cent. A great political revolution is in progress, and the Democratic, Conservative, specie-paying party are coming into power. Then Uncle Sam may liquidate the debts of his thirty-seven boys, and advertise to all the world that "he will pay no more debts of their contracting." Federal Four per Cent. Bonds of about £80,000,000 will wipe out all these State obligations, which would be worth more than a thousand millions to American credit in Europe. What an era of good feeling such a magnanimous policy would inaugurate!

STOCK EXCHANGE GAMBLERS.

SWINDLING on the Stock Exchange has become a science, and men engaged in "Bulling" and "Bearing" rascalities are considered respectable. They live in fine houses, keep costly carriages, own pews in fashionable churches, mumble orthodox creeds, and confess themselves "miserable sinners," which means that they regard themselves as the saints of the Lord, born to "inherit the earth." It is about time that these respectable criminals should be exposed and held up to the public infamy they so richly merit. The propensity to gamble is an inherent attribute of human nature; and in no country of the world is the gambling passion more fully developed than in England. Parliament adjourns on the Derby Day, the great national holiday devoted to gambling on horse-speed. But England, with hypocritical inconsistency, will not license a gambling house, nor permit a penny toss-up in the streets, or a bet for a "bob" in a public-house, although "gentlemen" may bet their fortunes at Tattersall's or at the Clubs. In view of the lying and cheating of the Stock Exchange, in which thousands of "respectable" men, including parsons, are daily engaged, the *Cosmopolitan* has the courage to "take the Bull by the horns," and the Bear by the tail, and denounce this public gambling as the greatest of public crimes. Better go to Monaco or Fontarabia, and sit down in an elegant room, in the company of well-dressed and well-mannered people of both sexes, and risk money on the turn of the *roulette* or the colour of *rouge-et-noir*. It is infinitely more pleasant, more honest, and should be considered more respectable, than the "cut-throat game" of the Stock Exchange. The most criminal feature of Stock gambling is the "selling short" system—that is, selling what one does not possess; and, in order to get hold of the article cheap, lying becomes a science. These "Bears," who stick at nothing to depress the quotation of the shares they wish to buy, might as well sell a man's house, or his horses, "short" as his shares in a mine or railway. In either case the property must be depreciated by false reports. Until Parliament passes a law prohibiting this iniquity, we see no remedy for it. And Parliament is not likely to pass any such wholesome law, as the majority of the members are up to their lips in Stock "transactions." As long ago as 1732, the evils of "time bargains" had become so manifold, that an Act, known as Sir John Bernard's Act, was passed, rendering all such bargains illegal, and enacting that every contract for the purchase and sale of stock which was not made *bonâ fide* for that purpose, but was made as a speculation on the fluctuation of the market, was void, and all parties entering into the same were liable to a penalty of £500 for each transaction. This Act was, however, shortly afterwards repealed. The Stock Exchange, like the Bank of England, owes its origin to the embarrassments of the Government shortly after the Revolution of 1688, and grew out of the practice of hawking the Government securities at various rates of discount in Change Alley. This gave rise to "stock-jobbing," which gradually became so thriving, that it required a settled place of business, whither those who were occupied in it might resort. From Change Alley the fraternity removed in 1773 to Sweeting's Alley, where a room was engaged, which was called the "Stock Exchange," in which any man might transact his business upon payment of the sum of sixpence. But the National Debt grew steadily, other Stocks increased, and the business of stockbrokers was proportionately augmented. At length, in May 1800, the foundation-stone of the first Stock Exchange was laid in Capel Court, where formerly had stood the residence of William Capel, Lord Mayor of London. From this time none have been admitted but members, who are elected by ballot, and pay an annual subscription of ten guineas. The members do not constitute a corporation of a joint-stock company, but form a voluntary association consisting of brokers and jobbers. The brokers act as agents for the purchase and sale of securities for the public, while the jobbers buy and sell on their own account. Recent developments in the City, and notably the Abbott-Labouchere fracas, and the "Eupion Fuel Fraud," are directing public attention to the enormity of Stock Exchange crimes; but the press treats the matter gingerly. One of the proprietors of the *Daily News*, a large " operator for a fall " or for " a rise," who swore before the Lord Mayor that he did not know the meaning of the word " Bear," doubtless " inspires " the money articles of his own newspaper. Hence these articles, written in the interest of an interested party, can have no value to the public. And this is but one specimen of Stock Exchange journalism. " City Editors " all get rich, and, Sampson-like, retire to elegant country seats to spend the "contingent remainder" of their successful lives. We heard a conspicuous Stock Exchange broker declare the other day that he would pay the "City Editor" of the *Times* £3000 a year to dine with him once a week, and to have the fact generally known in the City. Again we advise all honest "speculators," desirous of "tempting fortune," to quit the Stock Exchange "Hell" and pack off to Fontarabia, where, comfortably seated before the *tapis vert* of M. Dupressoir, they may pocket their gains and losses with the satisfaction of knowing that, whichever way the "luck" may run, there is no lying or "cheating around the board."

MONEY, BRAINS, AND MANNERS.

"Some people has plenty money and no brains, and some people has plenty brains and no money." Such was the shrewd reflection and execrable grammar of the vagabond butcher when meditating the most impudent fraud the world has ever witnessed. It suggests, however, the recognition of an universal fact, of which we are constantly reminded — plenty of brains and no money, plenty of money and no brains. The union of these two excellent commodities are but the rare exceptions. We know that men who have suddenly acquired or tumbled into wealth are apt to flatter themselves that "brains has done it." On the contrary, in nine cases out of ten, the lack of brains may have done it. Men of large intellect, the immaterial product of brains, are generally occupied in the pursuit of something better than mere riches. With their eyes on the stars, they do not see the pennies to be picked up at their feet. The greatest men of all ages have been proverbially the poorest men, while the Christian apotheosis of humanity was a houseless, homeless pauper, who "had not where to lay His head." Far be it from us to deprecate the possession of wealth. Money is a very convenient thing to have in the house, and fortunate is he who has never touched, and never fears to touch, his "bottom dollar." And yet there are many men with unlimited fortunes and very limited brains, who make mere wealth offensive by the "airs" they take in consequence of its possession. A vulgar, purse-proud man or woman is one of the most contemptible nuisances in existence. In themselves absolutely nothing, they assume enormous consequence from the fortuitous accident of a large bank-account. Ill-born, ill-bred, ill-mannered, and ill-looking, they swell to bursting on the possession of an adventitious attribute which "perishes in the using." How many of these empty-headed, plethoric purses are met in society as "honoured guests," where, stripped of wealth, they would not be accepted as servants! Let us "point our moral" with an anecdote in illustration of vulgar wealth. At one of our West End hotels there arrived a few days since a certain American lady, who demanded a room with an air that smacked of "sovereignty." The manager replied that the hotel was full to overflowing. "But I will have a room," shouted Madame Shoddy. Somewhat startled by the emphasis with which this declaration was uttered, the manager said he had only one parlour unoccupied, and that belonged to a gentleman who would be out of town for a few days. If the lady would take it on the condition of giving it up when the gentleman returned, she might do so. The room was accepted. A few days afterwards Mr X., who had occupied the apartments for more than two years, returned, and, on going to his parlour, found Madame in possession, who, with a grand imperious air, forbade his entrance. But, Madame," the gentleman remonstrated, "there must be some mistake, these rooms are mine; you will see my monogram on all the books and pictures, and I have occupied them for more than two years." "I don't care if you have occupied them eighty years," said her ladyship. "My husband is the *richest man in New York;* and if he were here, he would kick you across the street!" The gentleman beat a hasty retreat in search of the manager, who came and politely reminded the irate woman of the conditions on which she was permitted to occupy the apartments—only until the return of Mr X. "*You lie!*" shrieked Madame, and the curtain fell. But the rightful "claimant" was soon in possession. Is it any wonder that the

P

snobocracy of America get sometimes severely criticised in Europe, and that money minus brains makes the vulgar millionaire a nuisance? On the other hand, money *and* brains, with a little love and beauty thrown in, make the most blissful of all marriages.

THE BIRD.

THIS is the simple, yet comprehensive, title of a great work on ornithology, by Jules Michelet. It is beautifully written, delicately and artistically illustrated, and altogether it is one of the most charming books, not only of "the season," but for all seasons, that we have ever read. No one can close this thoughtful volume without being in love with the darling little birds, and Him who made them. Michelet devoutly believes that birds have souls, and, after carefully considering all his arguments, observations, and anecdotes, we are not disposed to dispute the theory, but shall henceforth regard every little bird we see on the earth or in the air as a *wingèd thought*. Birds certainly love, and plan, and reason. They also have a language of their own, and communicate ideas and emotions to each other. As builders of nests, or homes in which to rear their young, the birds are unsurpassed in ingenuity even by man. With nothing but claw and beak and breast to procure materials and shape their little cradles, the nest of the "humming-bird," for instance, is a marvellous piece of architecture; and so is the woodpecker's a work both of architecture and sculpture. And when it comes to music, no human *prima donna* has ever yet equalled the rich, voluptuous, and varied song of the nightingale. We deliberately use the word *varied*, as the miraculous music of this "soul of melody" is never the same, but an infinite variation and amplification on the eternal theme of Love, which we take to be the keynote of creation. The highest compliment ever paid to a great singer is to call her a "nightingale." It made one celebrated Italian *cantatrice* weep to be thus saluted by the peasants of Russia. In teaching their little ones first to fly and then to sing, the bird exhibits something more than what we vaguely call instinct. The patient lessons are given by "precept and example too." In the East, young nightingales, tamed, are taken to a regular singing-school, and placed in a room where a famous old singer gives them practical lessons, and his attentive little pupils soon become experts. But why does this strange bird, of unattractive form and plumage, sing in the night? Is not the day long enough to exhaust the flood of melody that swells in his little bosom, aching with joyful pain or painful joy? The lark, that "singing up to heaven's gate ascends," bursts into music at the first touch of light, and never utters a note in darkness. But the dear little

> "Nightingale, that all day long
> Has cheered the village with his song ;
> Nor yet at eve his note suspended,
> Nor yet when eventide is ended,"

makes even midnight darkness seem luminous with the gushing melody of his sweet-toned music. Is it joy or sorrow that inspires the lay? Sometimes it makes us weep, sometimes it makes us glad; but that depends not so much on the tones of the singer as on the mood of the listener. "There's not a bonnie bird that sings," says Burns, "but minds me o' my Jean;" and not only the soul-entrancing music of the nightingale, but the "home-notes" of all other birds are fraught with plaintive associations. The short, sharp notes of the swallow that twittered under the eaves of the old homestead; the mournful repetitions of the robin that sang and rocked on the willow that wept over a mother's grave—we can never hear these touching tones in any land, or under any circumstances, without a momentary moistening of the eyes, and a wish that we too had wings to fly away from the approaching winter, and be at rest. Thank God, since the age of thirteen we have never killed a bird but once, and that was a duck for dinner. And we wish all our little brother and sister birds to know the fact!

LIFE AMONG THE MODOCS.

"LONELY as God, and white as a winter moon, Mount Shasta starts up sudden and solitary from the heart of the great black forests of Northern California." With this lofty sentence, the keynote of a prose poem, well sustained to the end, Joaquin Miller opens his "Life Among the Modocs," the author of which will not only be known hereafter as the "Poet of the Sierras," but as the friend of the Red Man, as the noble old Indian Chief Logan is known as "the friend of the White Man." The book is fitly dedicated to the Red Men, and we do not hesitate to pronounce it the best work on the North American Indians ever written. The author lived among them, loved them, and understands them better than any "pale face" who has ever abused or defended them. Near the close of the volume we find this solemn sentence—" When I die, I shall take this book in my hand, and hold it up in the Day of Judgment as a sworn indictment against the rulers of my country for the destruction of these people." Miller evidently differs from Bret Harte, who declares that "Injins is pisin." Great injustice has always been done to these aboriginal tribes. Neither Cooper's pen nor Catlin's pencil has depicted the "noble savage" as he was and is before his contact with the White Men, before his demoralisation by fire-water and missionaries. From the day that brave Old Samoset shouted "Welcome Englishmen!" on the Hill of Plymouth, the poor Indian has been the prey of Anglo-Saxon cupidity. Few figures in history stand out grander or nobler than that of King Philip of the Narragansetts, who fought so bravely and died so gloriously on Mount Hope, in Rhode Island, where his ancestors had reigned for thousands of years. But no sooner is the Indian touched by civilisation than he imbibes all its vices and loses all his virtues. Originally he is proud, brave, and just. He will not turn on his heel to save his life, nor tell a lie to save his empire. But having been once tricked, cheated, and betrayed by his pale-faced enemies, he cheats and betrays in his turn, although he is no match for the subtleties of Christian treachery, for men with whom trade is a swindle and deception a life-long profession. In this "Life" by Miller, who has penetrated farther into the interior of Indian character, customs, and history than any other author we know, we have quite a new picture of the "noble savage" in his primeval home—pictures of Red Men who have never seen a missionary, never tasted fire-water, never learned to lie. And these are very unlike those miserable wretches lounging on the borders of civilisation, so graphically described by Train in his famous parody on the Pawnees, who, when they get a pair of old breeches, cut the bottom out and mount them—

"Lo, the poor Indian, whose untutored mind,
Clothes him before, and leaves him bare behind!"

These are the "noble specimens" of the vanishing Red Race one sees from the car-window all along the line of the far Western Railways; but they are very unlike those majestic "lords of the soil" who live under the shadows and ever-changing glories of Mount Shasta. But of all this there is a treat in store for the readers of this great book. While we have no reason to doubt the author's facts, and quite agree in his conclusions, we cannot shut our eyes to the poetic glamour and romance which illumines every sentence and magnifies every act. His heroes are—himself, "the Prince," and a beautiful young Indian girl—Paquita. As for "the Prince"—Colonel James Thomas—who happens at this moment to be in London, the author is absolutely in love with him; and if there is no exaggeration in the good deeds attributed to him, "the Prince" is indeed a rare fellow, and worthy of all admiration. We can only say, from personal acquaintance, that his appearance is "a combination and a form" to make women mad and men jealous; and his, also, is a character, as they say out in those wild "diggins," to *tie up to.* There is another character in the book, "a nearer and a dearer one," about which the author says but little. "Communication is sometimes blasphemy;" but he opens his heart just enough to let us see what and *whose* child occupies it—the beautiful half-breed girl now at school in San Francisco, learning catechism and coquetry among her White sisters. No doubt Tennyson's lines had something to do with Joaquin Miller's flight into the wilderness—

> "I will take some savage woman;
> She shall rear my dusky race."

This book is making a great sensation in England, and will have a wide sale, even at 16s. a copy. It is elegantly issued by Bentley, and is already in the hands of all the dukes and duchesses in the United Kingdom. It has given us one pleasant Sabbath, even in the dreary solitude of a London hotel. We advise everybody to read it. Nothing fresher or more vigorous has yet appeared from the American wilderness. It makes a modern "society novel" seem impertinent.

DISPOSAL OF DEAD BODIES.

THERE is a widespread agitation going on just now as to the wisest mode of disposing of dead bodies. Sir Henry Thompson's recent articles on the subject have excited a profound, and, we may add, a painful interest; for, to the least sentimental mind, either the burying or the burning of human corpses is a matter of the saddest reflection. Hard as it is, we must treat the question purely as a sanitary and economical one. The eye of the living must not linger on the body of the dead, nor imagination follow the slow and ghastly changes of the tomb. We turn away from the grave of a dear friend with a sigh and a shudder, resolved only to recall the form and features of the dead as they appeared when warm with life and radiant with love. And thus departed friends become sacred and immortal memories; and the longer we live, the richer is our mental picture gallery. As it matters not to the insensate body whether it is quickly reduced to a handful of ashes, or buried beneath the ground, to " lie in cold obstruction and to rot " for years and ages, it is the duty of society to consider only two things in disposing of it. The first is a question of public health, and the other one of mere economy in time and money. On these grounds the argument is all on the side of Cremation. Graveyards are not pleasant to look at as landscapes, nor to contemplate as receptacles of corruption. There can be no doubt that deadly gases, escaping from shallow graves, have often bred miasmatic fevers. Again, the cost of burial is a serious item in domestic expenditure, especially as extravagance in coffins keeps pace with extravagance in everything else, and that, too, with the least possible excuse for such ironical ostentation. We cannot blame a man for liking to live in a fine house, to ride in a comfortable carriage, and to wear nice clothes; but the money invested on silver-nailed and gold-plated coffins is not only a piece of wanton extravagance, but a dead loss to the world. Therefore, on the score of economy, funerals, coffins, and graveyards should be abolished. Of course the great army of undertakers will fight hard against the innovation, and black plumes and professional " weepers " will be at a discount. In fact, these useless, not to say odious, pageants have been going down ever since Charles Dickens held them up to public ridicule. They encumber

the streets with their sable omnibuses that never
bring a passenger back, and are altogether hideous.
Cremation will do away with all these useless and
unsightly spectacles. And then the land in all
large cities, always increasing in value, can be
put to much better use than by fencing it off into
graveyards, where Dives competes with Dives in
the costliness of his monument and the falsehood
of its inscription. Besides, if the Earth we in-
habit should last 50,000 or 100,000 years longer,
it will become one huge and pestilential graveyard,
and there will be no living in it, while all the
riches of the planet will be invested in coffins and
tombstones! But this is a consideration not
directly interesting to the present generation, and
only remotely concerns posterity; and posterity,
always equal to the occasion, will, doubtless, take
care of itself. In the meantime, there is a burning
fever to be burnt simultaneously raging in London,
Paris, and New York. In the latter city a public
meeting has been held, a Cremation Society organised, and candidates are sending in their names
as being desirous of *post-mortem* submission to the
crucible. Various inventions are coming forward
as the quickest and cheapest means of reducing
corpses to ashes, and we are daily expecting to
hear of furnaces in full operation. Urns will also
be in great demand for preserving the sacred

cinders. Each family, perhaps, may want a pattern of its own, with the customary coat of arms. There is some danger of a little extravagance in this business. Probably a glass vessel, without orifice, on which an epitaph could be neatly engraved, would be the best receptacle for the ashes. These relics could be kept in the *sanctum sanctorum* of the household; and when families emigrate to distant lands, there would be no more lamenting, on leaving the " graves of their ancestors "—

> " And where our fathers' ashes be
> Our own may never lie."

This is one of the saddest wails in Byron's "Hebrew Melodies." Cremation will spare the future all such heart-rending reflections. The *modus operandi* of burning the dead we will not describe to-day. The subject opens a new field for scientific investigation, and changes the occupation of gravedigger to fireman. But no human eye should ever be permitted to look into the oven during the transformation of the corpse into ashes.

CHURCH AND THEATRE.

THE Theatres of London are very crowded; the Churches are very thin. In the latter, people often go asleep; in the former, seldom. Theatres are open six nights in the week; Churches one day in seven. Admission to the Church is free; to the Theatre one has to pay more or less to enter. It is calculated that about 50,000 persons nightly attend the London theatres during nine months in the year. From these facts we infer that the public like the Theatre better than the Church. And yet Religion, to which the Church is dedicated, is a universal instinct, almost as strong as the sentiment of love. How, then, shall we account for this popular apathy, this general indifference to the Church? Our answer is, that the Religion to which the Church ministers is a sham Religion, a counterfeit, which the common instinct of humanity rejects, as naturally and as wisely as the palate rejects injurious food. The Established Church is an arbitrary institution. It has not life enough in itself to go alone. The Church of England has become a soft asylum for dainty Sybarites. Look at your luxurious Archbishop in palace and purple, with his £10,000 a year. Then think of the character and career of the poor Carpenter's Son, the humble plebeian, the meek and lowly Jesus, who had not where to lay His head! The State assesses a tax to support the Church, and the people pay because they must. Going to Church is enforced by the priests, who live sumptuously by pleading for the subsidised Establishment as " a duty." Some obey the mandate through fear, others because it is deemed respectable or fashionable, and others still from even less worthy motives—to exhibit their vanities in the shape of fine dresses and grand equipages. They do not go to the Church for instruction, as they always hear the "same old story;" nor for amusement and distraction, as to the Theatre. No doubt many "miserable sinners" endeavour to soothe their consciences by trying to believe that by going to Church they have " done a duty," atoned for some sin, or made themselves or somebody else better. But no logical mind can ever be the victim of such childish delusions. Church-going is not religion—it is not even morality. On the contrary, as a general rule, it is "the Devil's pet sin—hypocrisy." Your inveterate modern Church-goer, who prides himself on his "regular attendance on the services of the sanctuary," is generally the very counterpart of the Pharisee of old, who "loved to pray standing in the synagogues, and at the corners of the streets, to be seen of men." In nine cases out of ten, you will find him flint-hearted, close-fisted, and self-righteous "overmuch." And yet the poor people, the toiling masses, to whom poverty has made life but a pilgrimage of penance, are compelled to pay a large percentage of their earnings to support an Establishment for the benefit of parasites and hypocrites! Jesus of Nazareth taught no such Religion as this. The founder of Christianity was neither Pope, Bishop, nor Priest, and enjoyed none of the "fat livings" of these pampered minions of the Church. He gloried in penury, and never would have eaten a full meal while his poor brother had none, nor have possessed two suits of clothes while another went naked. Such is the humane and holy religion of Christianity, and it requires no puffs of the priesthood, no bellows-blowing of the Church, to fan the sacred flame. Taxing the people to support Religion is like pinching a woman to make her love you. The sentiments of the human heart are not to be forced, neither towards God nor towards man. No offering is acceptable that is not spontaneous. Instead of incense, it is simply an insult. Shock as it may the hirelings of the Establishment, we respectfully suggest that all Churches should be converted into Academies, and all priests into schoolmasters and nurses, with salaries, just sufficient to feed them wholesomely and clothe them comfortably. *Then* they might with some consistency call themselves the "followers of Christ." *Now* they only insult the name by such false pretensions. In the meantime, we venture to remark, that Temple-building is a relic of heathendom. The time for erecting monuments to the gods is past. All we want now is the school-house, the lecture-room, the laboratory of science; and, we will add, the Theatre. Yes, the much-abused Theatre—abused both by its friends and by its foes, although in different senses of the word. As an institution of instruction and amusement, the Theatre is sadly abused. It is far below what it might be and should be; and yet it must be regarded as one of the amenities of society, one of the blessings of social life. Many a weary heart and overworked brain finds distraction and consolation in the mimic drama of the stage. In the simulated sorrows of others, we, for the moment, forget our own—

> "When by the mighty actor wrought
> Illusion's perfect triumphs come,
> Verse ceases to be airy thought,
> And sculpture to be dumb."

THE SOLAR SYSTEM A SUCCESS.

WE have heard chronic grumblers grumble at almost everything, but we have never yet heard the shallowest atheist or the sourest cynic find fault with the Solar System. None of all these human growlers and grunters, who are never satisfied with the weather, or with anything else, unless, perhaps, in the midst of some gluttonous enjoyment, dares to impeach the economy, the accuracy, the noiselessness, and the beauty of the grand machine we call the Universe, or to impeach the skill and the power of the Great Engineer who "runs" it. All the movements of the heavenly bodies "come to time," thus proving the Solar System to be a system of pure mathematics, while the revolutions of planets, stars, and suns accord with musical exactness. That the "morning stars sing together" is something more than a figure of speech. Since Time began there has not been a collision, a jar, a discord among all the "heavenly hosts" that pay allegiance to our "Sun," nor among all the countless suns or stars that revolve in silent harmony around a still grander central orb. Truly it has been said, "An undevout astronomer is mad!" And yet, in the face of all this infinite grandeur, ineffable beauty, and everlasting beneficence, we hear of atheism and of atheists! The idol philosopher of England, John Stuart Mill, with whose eulogiums the newspapers are filled, and to whom a monument is about to be erected, is a confessed atheist! Here is something we cannot understand. In this pious, church-going, temple-worshipping England, where the Deity is recognised in every breath, and the name of God "written on the bells of the horses," the atheist Mill is held up as the greatest thinker, the most logical writer, the model philosopher of the age. Why, even a child, if you show him a watch, or a steam-engine, or a telegraphic apparatus, and tell him *the machine made itself*, would feel that the first ray of his reason was mocked. It strikes us that an atheist, a denier of a First Cause, supreme in knowledge, power, and beneficence, is simply an impossibility, who can no more frame a logical argument than we can build a pyramid by beginning at the top. That no two minds can have the *same idea* of the Deity we can readily understand, as no two minds are constituted alike, any more than any two bodies. Some admit a Deity possessing knowledge and power, but not beneficence. They believe in a great but not in a good God—a Being all intellect and no heart. This is the lamentable conclusion of misanthropes, with whom "everything goes wrong in the world," who curse the day they were born, and who have been goaded into rebellion and defiance by the monstrous, blasphemous doctrine of "eternal damnation." In plain English, men hate God because they have been taught to regard the Creator of the Universe simply as a Being endowed with supreme power and human passion. We hear of the "wrath" of God, the "anger" of God, the "sword" of God; and all such blasphemous nonsense is simply an insult to the serene and infinite One—the original and eternal Code of Laws that rules the universe "without variableness or shadow of turning"— One to whom all things are possible but the abrogation of His own laws. An instant's suspension of the laws of gravitation, and the whole Universe would be a wreck. Who, then, can believe that at the command of that semi-barbarous General, Joshua, the "sun stood still," in order that he might prolong his bloody battle in the valley of Ajelon? It was only a military division carrying the banner of "the Sun" that halted on that memorable occasion.

THE GILDED AGE.

WE are indebted to Mark Twain and Charles Warner for a work in three volumes, which we have devoured at a sitting. The fiction is founded on fact, and there is a sting of satire in almost every sentence. The characters are not caricatures but realities, and the more prominent ones will be easily recognised. " Weed " is Boss Tweed, and " Senator Dilworthy " is Senator Pomeroy—" Old Subsidy Pom.," as he is familiarly known in Washington. We quite agree with the following criticism in the *Standard:*—" It is a bitter pill for Americans to swallow; but the medicine is, in the judgment of its authors, a necessary one, and it is not for Britishers to disagree with them. Every line of the work can find a parallel in the New York press alone; every incident seems so real to those who know the States, that it might have been clipped from contemporary records; and some of the characters are less caricatures than touched photographs, notably those drawn in connection

with a murder case described in the third volume.
The object of the authors has been to draw a
terrible picture of over-speculation in business, of
corruption in the Senate and in the Court-house,
and of the rule of the mob; and they have only
too thoroughly succeeded. To call the 'Gilded
Age' merely a novel is to say little for it. It is
a heliotype in which the shadows are hardly
blacker than they are in nature, and in which
there are very few 'high lights' at all. It is a work
which, however, every one should read, and which,
when read, must make the world wonder how the
Americans could have ever objected to a single
word in 'Martin Chuzzlewit.'" We have no
doubt the Americans will swallow the "pill" with
great avidity, and it will do them good. As they
are shown up by their own pet artists, they will,
probably, to quote their own language, "acknow-
ledge the corn." The speculating, gambling,
reckless spirit of the age is depicted to the life;
and all the scenes—the race on the river, the
laying out towns in the West, the lobbying
at Washington, and the murder trial in New
York, read like fresh reports in yesterday's newspaper. The fictitious portion of the book seems
the least fictitious of all. Poor "Laura Hawkins,"
who fascinates everybody who sees her, is another
Laura Fair of San Francisco fame. The boat-race

and explosion on the Mississippi is but the report, in most graphic language, of an actual occurrence. "Colonel Sellers," a victim of hope, ambition, and poverty, is a character one meets every day in America, and occasionally in Europe. That dinner he gives out West, when the bill-of-fare is limited to raw turnips and water, is a picture worthy of the pencil of Hogarth. Another touch of nature is given in the description of the bursting, patriotic backwoodsman, who always, before going to bed at night, went outside of his cabin door and lifted up his voice to the woods around in the song of "The Star-Spangled Banner." He couldn't "keep" till morning without giving vent to his expansive enthusiasm. But about the best thing in the book is the report given, phonetically, of the old nigger's prayer when he first sees a steamboat rounding a point on the Mississippi River one moonlight night, and thinks "God A'mighty's coming for him." The first ejaculation is, "Heah I is, good Lord." And then he pleads stoutly for the "innocent chil'n." "Take dis old nigger, deah Lord, but spare dese innocent chil'n." Finally he begins to plead for himself, and suggests that there are other old sinners about, "full of cussedness," which the Lord had better take than himself—"poor old Uncle Daniel, who hasn't long to live, anyhow." There are also very serious, very profound, and painfully pathetic chapters in the book. "Si Hawkin's deathbed" will bring a misty sensation to the eyes of those who have a heart of flesh, and who know what the "first dark day of nothingness" means—when the pleasant voice is hushed, the light of the eye extinguished, and the form we loved to embrace lies cold and still in death. The book is profusely illustrated, which adds vividness and reality to the characters and scenes so powerfully portrayed by the pen. Notwithstanding the high price at which the book sells in England—some seven dollars—it will, doubtless, be in great demand at the libraries. In the meantime, perhaps Tauchnitz will give us a cheap edition for the benefit of the million. Personally, we feel grateful to the authors of this admirable book. During the twenty-four hours that made up the last Christmas Day, it rendered us oblivious to the vast loneliness of a vast hotel, with all its guests merrymaking in the country; and, better still, relieved us of that—

"Sorrow's crown of sorrow—
The rememb'ring happier things,"

as our laurelled poet sings.

LIFE OF JOHN OF BARNEVELD.

ANOTHER monumental work from the industrious pen of John Lothrop Motley. But who was John of Barneveld? will be asked—a name almost unknown at the present day? He was Prime Minister of the United States of the Netherlands two hundred and fifty years ago, and king in all but name. James was then on the throne of England, Henry IV. reigned in France, and Philip in Spain. The Puritan Fathers of the New World were sojourning at Delfthaven, preparing to embark in the *Mayflower*. The epoch was one of extraordinary interest, and John of Barneveld, called the "Advocate" of the Dutch Republics, was one of the grandest and most conspicuous diplomatists of his time. Mr Motley, the truly great American historian, with patient, heroic industry, has dug out his materials for these two noble volumes from the time-stained manuscripts, almost illegible, in the archives of Holland, and the work forms a fitting sequel to its illustrious predecessors from the same pen. We have read it with more interest and satisfaction than we know how to express. The style is simply perfection, and the philosophy is equally admirable. The author, in connection with the biography of his hero, discusses great questions of government, of religion, of war, of diplomacy, and of personal character. In no other book have we found sharper or wiser criticisms of Elizabeth, of James, of Henry IV., of Marie de Medici, the Prince of Orange, and of all the prominent actors in that remarkable era known as the "Thirty Years' War," but which, in reality, raged for eighty, between Catholics and Protestants, and then between the various quarrelsome divisions of Protestants. In those grim days, men went to war on the question of Predestination and Infant Damnation, and cut each other's throats in "defence of the Faith." King James, who claimed to be sole "Defender of the Faith," and who persecuted the Puritans in England, and those who persecuted Puritans in Holland, insisted that one man was born to be saved, another to be damned, and that "hell was paved with infants' skulls." And so did Maurice, the warrior Prince of Orange. Hence a century of war, the causes and the consequences of which Mr Motley traces with the most logical lucidity in his Life of Barneveld. As we have not space enough to quote from this admirable book—a book not for a day but for all time—we can only commend it to our readers as a study and a pleasure, worth whole libraries of so-called " modern literature." Motley, Bancroft, and Prescott are the three great historians of the present century— three "immortal names, that were not born to die."

INDEPENDENT JOURNALISM.

INDEPENDENT journalism is as rare as disinterested charity, and far less profitable. Let the reader name an English newspaper, if he can, that represents anything more than the prejudices, the traditions, the caprices of political parties, religious sects, literary cliques, social circles, and vested interests. In fact, newspapers are generally started for the sole purpose of supporting special objects, social, financial, political, or religious. They must be both partisan and sectarian, out and out, in order to gain the support of some particular sect or party. We look in vain in the one-sided columns of any of the great London newspapers for the spirit of freedom, of independence, of impartiality. To begin with the *Times*, the great misleader of British public opinion. The syndicate of Printing House Square, which controls the voice of the "Thunderer," is an organic body of insular prejudice, devoted exclusively to the interests of the *Times*, and to the gratification of personal, political, and national spleen. Let a public man offend it, and his name is tabooed from its columns, no matter how famous the name may be. When Boucicault, the celebrated dramatist and actor, incurred and defied its wrath, his name was ostracised from its columns "for two years, and those the most prosperous years of his life." And yet the *Times* claims to be a newspaper! Another instance of *Times* bigotry. A few years ago a certain New York journalist published a book anonymously, which had a large and rapid sale, and, of course, was generally " noticed " by the Press. The London *Times*, having received a copy of the work, ordered it to be reviewed by one of its literary hacks, who gave the book a long and laudatory article, which was "already in type," when the magnanimous manager, on discovering the real name of the author, ordered the article to be cancelled! But we have a fresh illustration of the personal spite of the *Times*. A few weeks ago, when the *Cosmopolitan* had the courage to apply to the "Claimant" the names of the felonies of which he had confessed himself guilty in the witness-stand, complaint was made to the Court against this journal for contempt. While all the other newspapers mentioned the name of the *Cosmopolitan* in connection with the case, the *Times*, with its characteristic prejudice, called it "a weekly newspaper." These are trifles, but they illustrate the fact that there is no independence, and very little fairness, in the spirit of British journalism. Every newspaper is the centre of a clique, with its pets to applaud, and its enemies to punish. These "Rings" of the Press seem to be only watching for an *apropos* to puff a friend or stab a foe. And when one of the latter category, who has not "bowed the knee to Baal," dares to write a book, to compose or sing a song, or to set up an independent newspaper, how eagerly and how unitedly they pounce upon him! He does not belong to our set; ostracise him. He is not of our political party; extinguish him. He belongs not to our Church; crucify him. This is the very essence of English journalism, of English criticism, of English justice. And the *Cosmopolitan*, which belongs to no sect, party, clique, or nationality, has the courage to say it. To put the matter a little more strongly, we assert our belief that if Gladstone or Disraeli were to write weekly leaders for the *Cosmopolitan, anonymously*, not a newspaper in London would notice them. Any old woman who "gives tongue" in the *Times* or the *Saturday Review* is listened to as an oracle.

THE GERMAN OCTOPUS.

PRINCE BISMARCK, the German Octopus, is feeling for a foothold in America. Since his triumphant subjugation and dismemberment of France, the ambitious Prime Minister of the Consolidated German Empire has manifested a disposition to compete for power with Russia in the East and with England in the West. His policy may be summed up in two words—expansion and domination. To this end Germany must become a great Naval Power, contending with England for the supremacy of the sea, and a great Financial Power, converting the bulk of the world's bullion into current coin bearing the " image and superscription" of Kaiser William. It is also necessary that Germany should emancipate herself from ecclesiastical dominion, looking to Berlin rather than to Rome for laws to govern the Church, as well as to guide the State. This is certainly a magnificent programme; and, admitting the great primary law of self-interest to be the highest of all human inspirations, we do not hesitate to call Bismarck a patriot, a lover of his country, *par excellence*. As for ability, and what the world calls statesmanship, we have not seen his equal in diplomatic audacity since the days of Talleyrand. And yet, with all his comprehensive cunning and scheming, the Prussian *intriguant* is in imminent danger of falling a victim to that "vaulting ambition which o'erleaps itself." Bismarck is provoking hosts of enemies both at home and abroad: most dangerous and most insidious of all are the Jesuits, whose sleepless animosity, the world over, like a woman's vengeance, is all the more fatal from the apparent weakness of the hand that strikes. The German States are consolidated by force, not welded by love; and States pinned together by bayonets are not likely to form a lasting Federation. Political discontent and religious antagonisms are seething throughout all the German Empire. It becomes necessary, therefore, to pick a quarrel abroad in order to maintain loyalty at home. As we have said, the German Octopus is now stretching his *tentaculæ* far over the sea to find a *point d'appui* in the West. In the lyrical language of Lydia, he is " the octopusest octopus that ever you did see." To become a great Naval Power, a rival to that expansive and heroic Power which for a thousand years has "ruled the waves," it is absolutely necessary for Germany to have naval stations and harbours in the Carribean Sea or the Pacific Ocean. Overtures have been successively made to St Domingo, to Porto Rico, and to Mexico; but thus far without success. Having failed to win or bribe any of these petty Powers to yield to his embraces, the Octopus has recently attempted to "accomplish his purpose" by violence on the virgin islands of Samoa, in the South Pacific, the "Dreamland" of which we gave our readers some account in a recent issue of the *Cosmopolitan*, based on the Report of Col. Steinberger to the State Department at Washington. During the last week telegrams have been flying across the Atlantic announcing the attempted rape by the Octopus, or, to drop the figure, of the appearance of the German war-steamer *Ancona* in Samoan waters, demanding a certain pecuniary indemnity of the natives, while threatening to "burn the Islands." The pretence for this hostile demonstration, as we happen to know, was based on a claim for 18,000 dollars, made by the house of Goddefroy & Co., of Hamburg, who for many years have monopolised the trade of the Samoan Islands, and amassed princely fortunes thereby. Herr Cæsar Goddefroy, a member of this firm, is also an influential member of the German Senate.

Hence this recent movement to subjugate the Samoans, and get possession of one of the finest harbours in the world. This little game of the great chess-player was suddenly checkmated by certain Americans, who paid the Goddefroy claim, when the Octopus pulled himself together and retired. Meantime the United States, who are going to annex these Islands at no distant date, has ordered the war-steamer *Tuscarora*, with Commissioner Steinberger on board, to make all possible haste to reach the Bay of Savaii, the capital of Samoa, and there unfurl the Stars and Stripes from the pinnacle of the loftiest mountain, in defence of the "Monroe doctrine." Colonel Steinberger, who has already been accepted by all the native authorities as Chief of the Islands, left Southampton on Saturday last in the Baltimore steamer *Ohio, en route* for the beautiful family of Nine Islands, forming the Samoan Group, in the Dreamland of the Pacific. Hundreds of millions of new materials will soon be added to the commerce of the civilised world.

PULLMAN ON THE MIDLAND.

THE English people, as a rule, are not much given to innovations. They are eminently conservative by nature and habit. A Government that has existed for a thousand years has educated the people into a general state of contentment—the state of Apostolic beatitude. "What was good enough for our fathers and our grandfathers is good enough for us," is the practical and comfortable creed of the average Englishman, not only in religion, philosophy, and politics, but in all the economies of social, industrial, and domestic life. Hence the proverbial difficulty of introducing a new idea into England. "John Bull don't see it," is the constant complaint of Americans who come here with their new-fangled notions. A very strong prejudice exists against everything *new*, no matter how long or how successfully the invention or discovery may have been in operation elsewhere. But there are exceptions to all rules, and one of the most signal exceptions of recent date is the adoption of the Pullman Car by the Midland Railway Company. These locomotive palaces, which have made travelling in America a luxury for the last fifteen years, are now running out of London to certain stations on the Midland Road, and will, doubtless, soon be adopted by all the other leading Lines. Twenty additional Cars are now on the way to Liverpool from America, and many more will doubtless follow. For the introduction of this great "improvement" the British public is indebted to James Allport, Esq., the General Manager of the Midland, of whom one of the leading Railway men in the United States said to us in New York, "He is the most intelligent Railroad man I have ever met." Mr Allport, after travelling extensively on the American Roads in the Pullman Cars, came to the conclusion that England could no longer afford to do without them. Arrangements were immediately made to introduce the Pullman on the Midland, on the same terms as in the United States. But this is not the only American idea adopted by Mr Allport for the comfort and security of the public. He has also introduced the Westinghouse Air-Brake, Miller's Patent Couplings, with improved springs, bogies, &c.; in fact everything which has been successfully tested on the other side of the Atlantic. In this respect the Midland Manager has shown himself to be a man above all insular prejudices— a thorough Railway cosmopolitan. Twenty-five years ago Mr Allport took charge of the Midland, then a single Line of about forty miles. It has grown up under his enterprising management to a system of Roads covering some twelve hundred miles, and the Company is one of the most successful in existence. The London Station at St Pancras, including the Midland Grand Hotel, is a magnificent embodiment of comprehensive ideas. The span of this superb structure is 243 feet from wall to wall, the length is 700 feet, and the height 100. The roof is 690 feet long, and the whole "shed" covers a space of nearly ten acres. Every iron rib in the roof weighs fifty tons. But the enterprising spirit of the Midland will not stop here. We understand it is in contemplation to open a ticket-office in London, where passengers, at their leisure, may provide themselves with tickets, *good until used*, and get their luggage "checked," as in America. The great convenience, and the saving of time and money, by this arrangement, will indeed prove a blessing to the travelling public. As the Company has already done so much in the way of increasing the facilities and comforts of travel on their Line, and shown such rare liberality in the adoption of American ideas, they cannot fail to reap their reward by a large increase of American patronage. It is estimated that not less than one million of dollars per annum is spent by Americans on the Road between Liverpool and London. Most of this money goes into the pocket of the North-Western, because that Line is the most direct, and a few minutes shorter. Having regard only to the pleasure and comfort of the traveller, we advise him to make this journey in a Pullman Palace Car on the Midland, which passes through the most beautiful and the most historically interesting part of England. Let him start, for instance, from London in the morning, and what a charming panorama is unfolded! The train leaves the ancient churchyard of St Pancras, where reposes the dust of the French Refugees; then passes the "Gospel Oak" of Haverstock Hill; across Finchley Common, where in 1660 General Monk massed his forces pending the Restoration of Charles II.; the famous pleasure resort at Hendon known as the "Welsh Harp," and the grave of Jack Sheppard; the celebrated Harrow School, founded in the reign of Elizabeth by John of Preston, who required each pupil to come provided with a bow and shaft, and where Lord Byron and Sir Robert Peel got their "rudiments;" on through St Albans, the ancient Verulam, where great battles were fought in the days of Julius Cæsar, and where the martyr Albanus was scourged and beheaded by pagan Britons; through the straw-plaiting village of Harpenden; past Luton Old Church, containing the beautiful baptistery presented by Queen Anne Boleyn; on by Dallow Farm, where, in the time of Charles, the Dissenters held their unlawful "conventicles;" through Bedford, where, in Elstow Church, John Bunyan "pulled the bell-ropes," and where, within the walls of the old gaol, he wrote that immortal book—"Pilgrim's Progress to the Celestial City;" past Oakley House, the seat of the Duke of Bedford; through Market Harboro', headquarters of the army of Charles I. before the battle of Naseby, and where Cromwell dated his despatches to Parliament announcing the defeat of the Royalists; Wistow Hall, where Charles stopped after the battle of Naseby; the historical town of Leicester, founded by King Lear, and where the great Wolsey died, a prisoner in the hands of the Duke of Northumberland, in the year 1530; and where, to-day, 15,000 stocking-frames are at work, supplying half the world with hosiery; Kegworth, where Tom Moore wrote some of his best poems, and where Heathcoat invented his bobbinet-machine;

on to Derby; a charming town, where we catch a glimpse of the spire of *All Saints' Church*, 174 feet above the pinnacles, erected in the time of Henry VIII., and where the Pullman Cars are put together; Belper, where Messrs Strutt employ more than 2000 hands in their cotton-mills; Wingfield Manor House, built by the Lord Treasurer Ralph Cromwell, in the time of Henry VI., and where Mary, "the hapless Queen of Scots," was held a prisoner in 1584; Darfield, in whose church-yard Ebenezer Elliott, the "Corn-Law Rhymer," is buried; Woodlesford, the birthplace of Darnley, husband of Mary Queen of Scots, who was blown to pieces by gunpowder in Edinburgh, two years after the marriage; Skipton, the home of the Cliffords, immortalised by Wordsworth; Kimbolton, where poor Queen Catherine, after her divorce, retired and died—

> "Shipwrecked upon a kingdom where no pity,
> No friends, no hope, no kindred weep for me;
> Almost no grave allowed me; like the lily,
> That once was mistress of the field, and flourished,
> I'll hang my head and perish."

Old Wisbeach, where William the Conqueror built a castle;—all these, and many other places of historical interest, are to be seen on the road from London to Liverpool from the Car windows on the Midland Line. Our Transatlantic friends should not fail to make this trip by daylight. The fare is the same, the comfort incomparably greater, and the route of such surpassing interest, that, instead of finding the few additional minutes wearisome, the traveller will find himself all too soon at the end of his journey.

THE AMERICAN CENTENNIAL.

WE consider it the patriotic duty of every man, woman, and child in America to contribute to the success of the coming Centennial Anniversary of the national independence of the United States. To preserve the national autonomy for a hundred years, triumphant over foreign foes and domestic rebellions, is certainly a record to be proud of. To have grown within this period from three States to thirty-seven, and from a population of three millions to forty, is a record of national prosperity utterly unequalled in the history of the world. To commemorate all these achievements, to return national thanks for all these blessings, the Americans have fixed on their hundredth anniversary, the year 1876, as a year of jubilee, and are making vast preparations for its appropriate celebration. Philadelphia, Penn's piously named "city of brotherly love," the "cradle of American Liberty," the "National Mecca of Freedom," is selected for the grand solemnities. The people throughout the entire Union have gone to work with an almost religious enthusiasm to get up the grandest International Exhibition the world has ever seen, and we do not hesitate to predict for this noble undertaking a success beyond the most sanguine dreams of the projectors. Some five millions of dollars have already been raised for the cause, and as much more will be freely forthcoming. If Congress does not see fit to make the appropriation, the voluntary and eager contributions of the people will provide all the means required to crown the edifice with unbounded success. Over twenty Foreign Powers have responded cordially to the invitation of the Washington Government, and manufacturers and producers from all parts of the civilised world are sending forward applications for space to exhibit their productions. As we announced some weeks ago in the *Cosmopolitan*, most of the European Governments will send Royal Commissioners to the Philadelphia Exhibition, many of whom will lend their choicest gems of art to grace the walls of the Great Picture Gallery. All that the world knows of science, art, and mechanism, will be concentrated for the benefit of the world in the Centennial Exposition of Philadelphia. The impulse this will give to trade and travel is too obvious for discussion. A hundred steamships will hardly be sufficient for the passengers and traffic across the Atlantic. New York will be inundated with European guests, as well as visitors from all parts of the United States, and the Railroad Companies will find the Year of Jubilee a golden harvest. Hotel-keepers within a radius of a hundred miles from Philadelphia are already preparing for the coming flood. There is probably not an American in Europe to-day who is not promising himself the pleasure of a visit to Philadelphia in 1876. The scattered children of the Republic will all flock homewards, like "doves to their windows," to swell the loud huzzas of the Year of Jubilee, the hundredth birthday of American Freedom.

EGYPT.

THE author of the "Hans Breitmann Ballads," who passed last winter in Cairo, has issued a volume entitled "The Egyptian Sketch-Book," but which, with commendable self-appreciation, he characterises, in one of the chapters, as "a Sketch-Book of Nonsense." Such modesty on the author's part may well disarm the critic. Mr Charles G. Leland has long ranked high among the witty writers of America : one of those desperately humorous fellows, who, like the poet Holmes of Boston, "do not dare to be as funny as they can," for fear of bursting the waistbands and corset-strings of their readers. In his Breitmann lingo of broken Dutch, Mr Leland made a decided hit. The "Breitmann Party" went the rounds of the Press, and was everywhere read with irrepressible laughter. Nothing more grotesque has ever appeared in that "line of literature." We have often smiled, all alone in the dark, at the following graphic description of a scene at that famous " Barty "—

> " I valsit mit Matilda Yane,
> She weigh two hunder pound ;
> And every time she gif a joomp,
> She make der vinder sound."

There are also touches of genuine pathos in the Ballads, which give Mr Leland the right to be called a poet. In this Egyptian *brochure* we have one of those serio-comic works which neither make us cry nor laugh; a sort of half-and-half mixture, which satisfies neither the sentiment of fun, nor the affectation of philosophy. The book is written somewhat in the strain of Mark Twain's " Innocents Abroad; " but we refrain from making any comparison between the two—in fact, there is no comparison. The chapters on Asses and Fleas are written in a vein of solemn research quite worthy of the subjects—one moment amusing, the next disgusting. The book is sprinkled with anecdotes, some of which are good, but the majority should be credited to Joseph Miller, Pasquin, or some other ancient party on whom has been pasted the jokes of ages. As a fair specimen of the author's trifling, we quote the following—giving as a key to the wit, that Pelican and Woodcock, who are thus " embalmed in amber," are head-waiters at the Langham :—

"They keep two pelicans at Shepheard's Hotel, in Cairo, while they have only one at the Langham, in London. The two, however, at Shepheard's, though large, are very lazy, while the one at the Langham is small, but very useful and active. The woodcock in Egypt, or what I ate for such, were miserable creatures; while, *per contra*, the best woodcock I ever met in my life was at the same hotel in London." The more serious part of the book is devoted to laudation of the Khedive, whom the author regards as the most enlightened Ruler in the world,—an estimation which we heartily endorse. Mr Leland well says—"With its railroads rapidly extending into a fertile country of enormous extent, inhabited by industrious and money-loving races, skilled in manufactures, and with a marvellously shrewd and vigorous man, of extremely liberal views, at its head, Egypt should not long remain a dependency; and until it is entirely free in every respect, it cannot enter as it should on the great career of progress." Since the death of the Third Napoleon, the Khedive of Egypt is the most advanced monarch living. And we believe the day of Egyptian independence is drawing near.

A GRAND COSMOPOLITAN ENTERPRISE.

THE Paris correspondent of the *Times* gave some encouraging and interesting items last week in regard to the proposed Nicaraguan Canal, which will be found reproduced in to-day's *Cosmopolitan*. It has long been a problem of the greatest interest to the commercial world, and, had it not been for the Civil War in America, no doubt this maritime connection between the Atlantic and Pacific Oceans would have been *un fait accompli* before M. Lessep's kindred undertaking of uniting the Red and Mediterranean Seas. This magnificent enterprise had a peculiar fascination for the late Emperor Napoleon, whose expansive and generous mind was always occupied with grand ideas; and we may state, that but for the disastrous German War, the Emperor would have given his powerful aid to the completion of the American Isthmus Canal. The cost of uniting the two great Oceans would be less than that of keeping the army of

France, or of the United States during the Rebellion, sixty days in the field. Peace hath her victories, and here is one in which all nations can unite for the common benefit of mankind. This inter-ocean Canal is not a national enterprise, but a truly cosmopolitan one. When first-class ships can come from San Francisco down the Pacific coast, cross the narrow neck between the two continents of North and South America, then up to New York, or on across the Atlantic, the Mediterranean, through the Suez Canal into the Red Sea, and out into the waters of the Orient, voyages round the world, for business or pleasure, can be made in less time than the famous "eighty days" of Jules Verne. And nothing is wanting to accomplish all this but one resolute human will. It was De Witt Clinton's will that married the waters of Lake Erie with the Hudson; it was De Lessep's energy that cut a pathway for ships through the Suez Isthmus; it was Field's persevering faith that placed Europe and America in instant electric communication. The will, the faith of one earnest man, can "remove mountains." And such a man, we believe, has taken hold of the Nicaraguan Canal question. Judge O'Sullivan is "the American" alluded to in the *Times* correspondence, who has set his heart and hand to the accomplishment of this great financial, commercial, and philanthropic work. Judge O'Sullivan is a man in the prime of life, of large experience in public affairs, who has represented the United States in France and in India, and been engaged in many successful undertakings in Mexico, where, during the brief and unhappy reign of the noble Maximilian, he "did the State some service." This gigantic engineering work could not be in better hands. The enthusiasm of the " promoter " ensures success. The undertaking is practicable, feasible, and most desirable—infinitely more so than that "work of supererogation," the proposed tunnelling of the Channel between England and France. Recent surveys give the length of the Nicaraguan Canal as about 181 miles, of which there is Lake navigation 56 miles, and River navigation of 63 miles, leaving only 61 for the actual cutting of the Canal, with the mean depth above the water of 30 feet. Only fourteen locks would be required to overcome the gradient of some 130 feet. It is proposed to make the Canal 72 feet wide, with a depth of 26 feet of water. The supply of water from Lake Nicaragua and the San Juan River is simply inexhaustible. As the San Juan forms a portion of the boundary between Costa Rica and Nicaragua, concessions would have to be obtained from both of these States, which are eager to see the work begun, as it will be of incalculable benefit, not only to the intersected States, but to the commerce of the whole world. As to the question of funds, we believe the sum total required to complete the work could be "syndicated" in a single day.

A RIGHTEOUS VERDICT.

NEVER has the common sense of justice—the noblest element in the human heart—been more profoundly satisfied than by the verdict and sentence given in the Court of Queen's Bench against the Tichborne Claimant, the most stupendous fraud the world has ever witnessed. There is only one regret among all intelligent, justice-loving minds, and that is the inadequacy of the punishment inflicted in proportion to the injury done. Eternity is not long enough for the full expiation of such a series of capital crimes as are involved in the false pretences, forgeries, libels, and scandals which have been deliberately invented and persistently perpetrated by this infamous, iniquitous, and callous Wapping butcher, who possesses far more of the nature of a hog than the character of a man, and whose infinite wickedness reconciles one to the doctrine of eternal punishment, the necessity of an orthodox hell. As the Judge remarked in pronouncing sentence, the law contemplated no such crimes as those committed by the Claimant in fixing the penalty for perjury. But the scoundrel is now about forty-four years of age, and the sweat of penal servitude for fourteen years, under the weight of such a monstrous mass of adipose matter, is about equal to a life sentence. If he should live through his term, and at the age of fifty-eight the monster should again be let loose on society, he will hardly be able to play another *rôle* of perjury and fraud, or to find accomplices, either men or women, to join him in new conspiracies. That there has been a most wicked and well-organised conspiracy admits not a shadow of doubt. It began in Australia as a money speculation, and it culminated in London with the same base motive. Is there no law, no punishment but public opinion, to reach the numerous accomplices of the Claimant? Kenealy should be disbarred, and the House of Commons should purge itself of Whalley. Onslow's constituents have already settled the question for him. But there are scores of others who took a conspicuous part in this brazen fraud, including Lord Rivers, Captain Brown, Luie, Bulpett, Miss Braine, &c., who deserve to share the punishment of the principal offender. It is no injustice to say that *some* of the above witnesses *knew* that the Claimant was an arrant impostor, and that they went into the witness-box for the deliberate purpose of committing perjury, and aiding the criminal in the accomplishment of his diabolical crime. The counsel for the defendant knew perfectly well from the opening to the ending of the case that their client was a fraud, and that every word they uttered in vindication of his innocence—to use a strong word—was simply *a lie*. The trial, extending over 188 days, and costing altogether not less than *half a million sterling* in cash, to say nothing of time, type, and patience, should not have lasted a week. The positive testimony of scores of witnesses that he was *not* Roger Tichborne, and that he *was* Arthur Orton ; that Tichborne was tattooed, and the man was produced in court who tattooed him; the elegant letters of Tichborne, compared with the vulgar scrawl of Orton—after submitting this indubitable and unanswerable evidence to the jury, the case should have been stopped, either by the jury, the Court, or the counsel for the defendant. The Claimant's conduct on the very first night of his arrival in London thoroughly identified him conclusively as Orton. With a dog's instinct he rushed back to the place where he was kennelled, and inquired for his old associates. Then he silenced, by bribery, his brother and sisters, inducing the former to change his name and place of residence ; and even after gagging them with Bank of England notes, did not dare to bring them into court. Circumstantial evidence like this, which is always stronger than direct *vivâ voce* testimony, is proof conclusive that the Claimant, now a convict in Newgate, is Arthur Orton and nobody else—a fact of which we have no more doubt than of our own existence. The summing up of the Lord Chief-Justice, already issued in one huge volume, is a monumental work, without an equal in the annals of jurisprudence. In argument, style, and temper, it will become a model of judicial administration, and a monument of judicial genius. The Jury, who have themselves been sorely tried in this case, have simply done their duty, as England expects every man to do his duty under all circumstances. But they deserve some public recognition for their patience, and the firmness they have shown through the trial, and by the prompt and explicit rendition of their verdict. And not the least do we honour them for giving official and emphatic expression to the universal indignation that has long glowed in every manly heart in Christendom at the most atrocious treatment of Lady Radcliffe by this infamous perjurer, who did his utmost to blast her character and ruin her happiness. As for Kenealy's "ministering angel," Miss Braine, who sat by the bedside and held the hand of this licentious and disgusting brute, after his foul charge against her former pupil, we do not think Mr Hawkins was any too harsh in the epithets he applied to her. This "angel"—an inverted one, we should say—swore that the Claimant was Sir Roger Tichborne, and that on the night he came of age she was governess in the house; and, fearing the young gentleman was getting a little too winey, she went up to his room, sent for him, and when he came to the door, *blew out the candle and pushed him in!* Rather presuming on the part of a modest governess, unless she wished to take advantage of Sir Roger's tipsiness. For the Tichborne bondholders, and the sporting crowd who have been betting, begging, and spouting in behalf of the Claimant, caring nothing for the cause of truth and justice, but only hoping to win their "odds," the public will have no sympathy. Henceforth, we trust, no witness will be allowed to open his mouth in the witness-box who has any pecuniary interest in the result of the trial in progress. The number of men, and women too, who will perjure themselves for money, as shown in the progress of this Orton fraud, is something appalling. As for the ragamuffin rabble, who have daily rendezvoused in Westminster to "cheer" the guilty Claimant and his not less guilty counsel, the verdict and sentence will perhaps convince them of the existence of the power of law and justice in England. The lesson, if duly digested, will prove a wholesome one to all rascaldom.

THE FUR COUNTRY.

ANOTHER marvellous and exciting mixture of romance and reality, from the prolific and powerful pen of Jules Verne, entitled "The Fur Country," has compelled us to read it from beginning to end before we could get the story "off the mind." It is an elegantly printed volume of 300 pages, profusely and beautifully illustrated, and containing in about equal proportions scientific knowledge and poetic imagination. The reader is kept on the constant *qui vive* to draw the line between the two. The scene of "The Fur Country" is correctly laid, and the history of the various "Companies" accurately given. The astronomy, geography, climate, and phenomena of the Arctic regions, including both land and sea, are depicted to the life, and in more vivid colours than we have ever found in the writings of Arctic navigators and discoverers. The Fauna and the Flora, also, of hyperborean latitudes are treated in the most exhaustive manner, and with technical precision. The author seems to be perfectly familiar with every star that shines, every flower that blooms, every fish that swims, and every bird that flies on the North American Continent from the Equator to the Pole, and at the same time discusses the habits of all the animals, ruminants, and rodents as thoroughly as if he had lived among them all his life. A wonderful *savant* is this M. Jules Verne, and we have to thank him for affording us more instruction and " entertainment" than we have found in books for many years. Nothing, since the adventures of poor " Robinson Crusoe," that jewel of the nursery, first inflamed our imagination, has more absorbingly " kept up the interest of the reader "—that is, of the writer—than these novel and fascinating productions of M. Verne, compounded of wonderful fiction and still more wonderful facts. We can see the little fellow alluded to across the background of fifty years, sitting in the corner of a huge New England fireplace, in the warm light of burning pine-knots, and devouring for the first time the story of Alexander Selkirk, rendered into a prose poem by the immortal pen of Defoe. The eager interest felt by that five-year-old boy in Robinson's romantic adventures is again revived by the still more romantic productions of this grand prose poet, who ties up the richest treasures of scientific knowledge with the rainbow ribbon of imagination. We heartily thank him for the transitory oblivion of cares and things around us his works have afforded, and still more for the revival of our childhood's faith in the "story" told us. And this, we consider, at once, to be an author's reward, and an author's object—to instruct and entertain his reader. To know that he has accomplished this end is a far higher satisfaction than any mere material compensation. "I sat up all night reading your book," said a lady once to an author who shall be nameless, "and it made me forget everything unpleasant and remember everything agreeable in my whole life." The author of that book felt that his work had not been entirely useless. But the debt of gratitude which the world owes to the authors of good books is too large a subject to be touched but incidentally. It is a theme worthy of an Academician's pen. To return to our charming "Fur Country," of which, by the way, we purposely refrain from giving any description. It is cruel to forestall curiosity in such a feast of surprises. The human characters introduced consist of a band of Fur-hunters, with the accidental addition of an English lady travelling for the sake of knowledge, and a Greenwich astronomer who is on his way to the 70th parallel of latitude to observe the eclipse of the sun in 1860. What perilous trials befell the expedition we do not propose to tell. Take the story either as all fact, or all fiction, the reader, who in childhood was thrilled by the adventures of the Scotch sailor in the Island of Juan Fernandez, will be spell-bound by these fearful scenes in the Arctic Regions. But we know that the work is grounded on reality. The "Fur Country" exists, and Fur-hunting is a real occupation, a great item of trade. As to the events described, the author is always pushing matters to the verge of the impossible. The long journey made on an island of ice taxes the belief of the most credulous; and yet, since the book was written, a somewhat similar voyage has been made by a portion of the crew of a late Arctic Exploring Expedition—the crew of the ill-fated *Polaris*, who floated on an island of ice fifteen hundred miles. And, after all, truth is stranger than fiction, and the realities of the world, both material and spiritual, far transcend the works of imagination. Whether it is wiser to believe everything or to believe nothing, we shall not venture to decide. The common experiences of life, the sad as well as the happy, may lead to either conclusion. We cannot quit the "Fur Country" without a word of admiration for the heroine, Paulina Barnett, a noble and a glorious woman. Not only admirable, but adorable. Is it possible that such a

> "Perfect woman, nobly planned,
> To warn, to comfort, and command,"

exists only in books? No, no, no! Full justice has never yet been done by pen of man to the "perfect woman," the exceptional woman, who, *rara avis in terris*, is still to be found in all countries, in all epochs, and under all conditions; a being in whom the "elements are so mixed" that beauty, goodness, sweetness, fidelity, truth, and love are the only possible results. Such is our ideal-real woman, whom Heaven's own angels cannot excel in loveliness—

> "Woman, whom God created with a smile of grace,
> And left the smile that made her on her face."

TALES OF THE STREETS.

WE have received a letter from Miss Stride, the good Sister of Mercy who devotes her life to the restoration of fallen angels, in which she says, "I read the paragraph in your last week's paper, 'Tales of the Streets,' and I now write to ask if you have any objection to my quoting it for a work I have long meditated doing, and which want of funds alone has prevented." Certainly not. Miss Stride continues: "It is my intention to build a large block of buildings, in which we shall be able to receive poor women such as you refer to. I propose keeping their children, and educating the girls for domestic servants, and the boys for soldiers or sailors; the mother to go into some situation as soon as her health permits, and help to support her children. I do not propose letting the father off free if I can find him. I have laid down my plans, but to carry them out I want £10,000. This sum will not do much more than buy the land and build the houses. I propose making a strong appeal to the people of England on behalf of this terribly neglected class of little children." This is truly a most excellent work, and should engage the hearts and hands of all who bear the name of Christians and claim the character of philanthropists. A hundred thousand women, of all classes and conditions of society, including wives, mothers, widows, and spinsters, nightly tramp the streets of London advertising the sale of their bodies for bread, while the Priests and the Levites go on begging for the rich Churches at home and the happy heathen abroad! These poor, despised, street-prostitutes are honest women in comparison with those " respectable " hypocrites, who do their " nest-hiding " in secret and deny it in public. Not having the good looks, or the good clothes, to exhibit themselves in the pig-market of Windmill Street, they have to wander and beg on the cold pavement. What the curbstone brokers are to the regular members of the Stock Exchange, these poor street-walkers are to the constant *habitués* of the Argyll Rooms. They manage these things infinitely better in Japan, or even in Paris or Hamburg.

LAW v. JUSTICE.

ALL civilised nations, and England not among the least, are afflicted with a mania for legislation. We live in a perfect maze of law. There is no end to it, and it by no means tends to further the ends of justice. Why not codify and condense the laws of nations into nutshells, into the Ten Commandments—the Code of Moses? There are but a few primary laws essential to the welfare of society, to the conservation of good government. The inalienable right to life, liberty, and the pursuit of happiness, is sufficiently protected by the great original laws—"Thou shalt not kill;" "Thou shalt not steal." These fundamental prohibitions are the bulwark of all social and governmental rights. The violation of these sacred laws should always be severely punished. It were well if legislation stopped here, or rather restricted all codes and forms of law-making to a mere amplification and application of these "first principles." As for tax-laws, we would abolish all but one—a direct *pro rata* tax on property. There should be no tariffs, no douane, no octroi impediments to trade and travel. But this irrepressible mania for law-making knows no bounds. Its restrictions are everywhere; and even Britons, with all their boasted liberty, are abject slaves to their law-makers, who interfere with all their domestic, social, and religious concerns. Take the Liquor Laws, Sunday Laws, Church Laws, School Laws, Marriage Laws, &c., for examples of this legal tyranny which justifies revolution. There is no personal freedom in an English Sunday. A stranger must walk the streets of London for hours before he can purchase a chop or a glass of wine. We must also perforce contribute to the support of a Church in which we do not believe, and to the education of other people's children. The Marriage Laws are, perhaps, the most despotic and oppressive of all. Men and women who have made the fatal mistake of selecting each other as companions for life, must be compelled to live together in spite of mutual repulsion and hatred, until one of the parties commits a crime to sever the knot! Repugnant unions lead only to endless wars and infinite miseries. Where the elective affinities do not exist, hell does. Marriage is a civil contract—which concerns only the parties who make it; and they who marry by mutual consent would be much more likely to live happily together to the end of the chapter, if they were free to dissolve the partnership by mutual consent. Of course, the husband should be compelled to support and educate his children, and his wife, too, so long as she remained true to him, whether under the same roof or not. Nothing but the wife's infidelity should absolve her husband from the moral and legal obligation to take care of her. The same law and justice should apply to what are termed illegitimate relations. According to the law of England, the father of an illegitimate child is condemned to pay the poor mother two-and-sixpence a week for a certain limited period. It strikes us that this is an outrage on woman, and an insult to justice. The father, in such case, should not only be compelled to support the child until it comes of age, but the mother also, until she find some other protector. But the subject opens too widely for full discussion in a newspaper article. We have rising before us whole catalogues of flagrant cases of law in conflict with justice, which we have not time even to mention to-day. These hints, however, may set some strong and earnest reformer to thinking on the urgent necessity of codifying, simplifying, and clarifying the great mass of laws which only serve to impede, not promote, the course of justice.

A CHALLENGE TO JACK FROST.

ANOTHER new American idea, which proposes to prevent canals from freezing. Mr Robert A. Chesebrough, a scientific New Yorker, has published a pamphlet giving full details of his plan for keeping the canals open during the winter by the introduction of artificial heat. Startling and impracticable as the proposition first strikes us, we are far from pronouncing the scheme impossible, or even visionary; and if the thing can be done, the importance of the invention can hardly be estimated in figures. It is a well-known fact that a body of water freezes only on the surface, and that it begins to freeze at 32° Fahrenheit. Mr Chesebrough proposes, by the insertion of a pipe filled with hot air running along the inside of the canal, to keep the water on the surface a degree or two *above* the freezing-point. If this can be done, the problem is solved, and we shall hear of no more commercial constipations by the closing of canals in winter. The great Erie Canal, for instance, which connects the Hudson River with Lake Erie, is closed for several months every year, and not unfrequently with millions of dollars' worth of produce locked up *in transitu*. In 1872 the canal transportation exceeded that of all the railroads. During the winter season, while the canals are ice-bound, the railways raise their freight rates some 300 per cent. During the winter of 1871, no less than four hundred boats, containing 3,500,000 bushels of grain, were frozen up in the Erie, the freight on which amounted to 640,000 dollars. Were it not for the ice embargo there would be a very great extension of the canal system in the Northern States. The Erie Canal would be extended to the town of Erie, where it would connect with the Pennsylvania Canal; thence to Cleveland, where it would connect with the Ohio Canal; thence to Toledo, where it would meet the Miami and Wabash Canals; and thence across the peninsula of Michigan to Chicago, where it would be united to the Mississippi River by the Illinois Canal. No one can for an instant doubt the vast importance of Mr Chesebrough's scheme. The only way to silence scepticism is to make an application of the theory on a small scale. If it prove successful, the inventor will have no trouble, even in panic times, in raising millions, if required, to keep all the canals, if not all the rivers, of the North open all the winter. The annual cost, as applied to the Erie, 350 miles, is estimated at 611,275 dollars— a mere bagatelle in comparison to the loss of freight receipts during the five or six frost-bound months of the year.

RETURN OF THE TIDAL WAVE.

The eternal and inexorable law of re-action was never more forcibly illustrated than by the recent elections in the United States. One of the great axioms of physical philosophy asserts that re-action is equal to action; and the pendulum never fails to swing back to the point from which it started. The mental or moral world seems to be governed by the same universal law. The flood of the tide will be equal to the ebb. Fourteen years ago the Black Republican party made a clean sweep over all the Northern States of the American Union, electing Lincoln President, and thereby causing the Secession War. It is true that Mr Lincoln was a "minority President;" but, while he received less votes than Douglas and Breckinridge, the two opposition candidates, he had enough to make him legally President, and the people submitted to the provision of the Constitution " in such case made and provided." The South, acting up to the menaces of the Presidential campaign of 1860, to secede in the event of the Black Republican party coming into power, confirmed their words by action, the month after Mr Lincoln's inauguration, by an attack on Fort Sumter, in the harbour of Charleston,—South Carolina being the first of the "wayward sisters" to raise the flag of rebellion, or independence as they called it down in Dixey. They were encouraged to take this step by a solemn "Resolution" passed by the Democratic Convention of the State of New York, at Albany, in February 1861, that the "Federal Government had no authority to coerce the action of a sovereign State." But for this "Resolution," which induced the South to believe that the great body of Northern Democrats would stand by them in the event of Secession, there would have been no War. Breckinridge, their recently-defeated candidate for the Presidency, had grandly declared that "the power to coerce resides nowhere." But we are writing of the solid facts of history, and not of the vain prophecies of politicians. In looking back upon the past, through the vanishing vista of three Administrations, and across the sad valley of half-a million of graves, without passion or prejudice, or the least bias of partisan feeling, we hold the Black Republican party responsible for the causes of the War and all its cost in blood and treasure, and for the millstone of Debt now weighing upon the neck of the nation. We only draw the indictment, and leave History to argue the case, establish the fact, and render the inevitable verdict. And now, at last, comes the reaction. The people will no longer be led into debt and destruction by a party of *doctrinaires* and political speculators. Abolitionism, a mere party shibboleth, a hobby to ride into power, is "played out." The nigger was emancipated through the exigencies of war, not from any conscientious pressure of "moral principles," and is now free to work, or beg, or starve. He is also endowed with the dangerous weapon of the franchise, with which to fight his white superior. In the meantime, the party in Power have ridden roughshod over the subjugated South, and "run the machine of Government" in the interest of the party, and of the particular pets of the party. We need not stop to call the long roll of "beggars on horseback" who, for the last ten years, have been revelling in wealth at the expense of the taxpayers. From the White House down to the smallest Custom-House, party officials have been "on the make," to use the slang phrase for official robbery and theft. And the stupid, patient masses, knowing all this, have borne it until now! At last they have waked up to a "realising sense of the situation," and the tidal wave of indignant reaction has swept mountains high, from Maine to Louisiana. Is it not grand, this spontaneous and majestic uprising of an oppressed people, determined—

"To right their wrongs, come weal, come woe,
To perish, or o'ercome the foe"?

From a majority of one hundred against them in the Federal House of Representatives, the Conservatives have an elected majority of over seventy. The dissolving majority of seven Republicans in the Senate will soon be reduced to zero, and a Conservative victory in the Presidential election of 1876 is a foregone conclusion. This is the most propitious "smile from the West" that has beamed on us since the dark War cloud shut from us the light of heaven and of home. The revolution is a most beneficent one, not only for the Union, but for "all the rest of mankind." The triumphant party, which is only conservative in comparison with the Radicalism and nigger-equality of Black Republicanism, is sufficiently progressive and pacific in its policy. Ostensibly, the Democrats are a free-trade, hard-currency, specie-paying party; but the Free Trade of all countries is a mere matter of personal and sectional interest. The American Democracy has its traditions, Jeffersonian, Jacksonian, and Bentonian, to which it still clings with commendable loyalty. It is eminently the friend of agriculture, and will legislate for the toiling million rather than for the luxurious millionaire. It prefers hard dollars, of fixed value, to filthy rags of fluctuating value, and of no value. It is not an agrarian party, but at the same time favours the general distribution of wealth, and not the massing of it into mountains for the benefit of "a moneyed aristocracy." It is emphatically the people's party, and an advocate of honest men and honest measures. It is not a pro-slavery party. *That* issue is dead and buried; but it insists that the white race is superior to the black. It is not an aggressive party, but it will not truckle to the dictates of Foreign Powers, and it will have Spain out of Cuba within thirty days from its installation at Washington; not to enslave the blacks, but to free them, and also the struggling whites of that always oppressed Island. Now, as a *per contra*, we give our readers the following brief sketch of the Democratic party, which appeared in the Philadelphia *Press*—in the absence of the editor-proprietor, be it understood—on the eve of the late election:—"It hung defenceless negroes to lamp-posts, and burned the asylums of innocent negro orphans in New York some ten years ago, and in 1871 the negroes of this city purchased their first ballots at the cost of the blood of their ablest and best leaders." Such electioneering stuff as this had much to do with the re-action that has overwhelmed the country. There is an eternal sense of justice deep down in the heart of all nations and all epochs, which neither the tyrants of the sword, the sceptre, nor the pen may outrage with impunity. And so the great "whirligig of Time brings all things even."

GOOD WISHES.

THE New Year, as usual, has brought the *Cosmopolitan* many good wishes from various parts of the world; and these are not unfrequently accompanied with friendly suggestions in regard to the business management of the paper. Being unable to answer all these kindly-meant communications individually, we propose to give a general reply, which, we trust, will be generally satisfactory. In the first place, let us frankly say that good wishes mean nothing unless backed up by more substantial support in the shape of a cash remittance — that is, from those who have the means. Not that good wishes and friendly sympathies are to be despised from those who have nothing else to give. This line of Burns is full of truth :—

"A man may tak' a neebor's part,
And ha'e nae cash to spare him."

But those who send us " good advice," and nothing else, and who perhaps spend hundreds a year on wine, women, and cigars—two of these three luxuries one can live without—but cannot afford to pay twenty shillings for fifty-two visits from the *Cosmopolitan*, must not expect to be entered in our books under the category of "friends of the paper." We recognise only two classes of people in the world—subscribers and non-subscribers; as poor Ada Menkin recognised only two classes of men—those who had married her and those who hadn't. We regret to say that the non-subscribing portion of the world still represents a considerable majority, although the disproportion is weekly diminishing. In regard to the suggestion from several true and substantial friends of the *Cosmopolitan*, that the paper should be regularly exposed for sale at all the railway stations and bookstalls in the United Kingdom, the United States, and in all the kiosks of Paris, our answer is brief: We tried it more than eight years ago, and it *didn't pay*. In the first place, that overgrown newsboy, W. H. Smith, whose rare thrift in his business enables him to attach M.P. to his name, holds a monopoly of all the English railway stations, and demands a price for allowing any newspaper to be sold at his stalls— Tribute, you see, sir, and no pun meant. Besides, he returns and exchanges all unsold copies for new ones, so that the publisher never knows what is coming back upon him in the shape of "waste." This is a kind of one-sided trade which we decline to be a party to. The publisher takes all the risk, and the vendor all the profit. No one, who really wants the *Cosmopolitan*, either one number or fifty-two numbers, can have the slightest difficulty in obtaining it, either by ordering it of a newsman, or by enclosing stamps or cheque direct to the office. The *Cosmopolitan* is not a cheap paper, or a trashy paper, or a sensation paper, and, consequently, it is not what is called a "popular" paper. We could not make such a one if we would, and would not if we could. The ragamuffins who run after Kenealy to cheer him, and after Hawkins to hiss him, would never buy the *Cosmopolitan* if it was for sale at every newspaper stall in England: the *Police News* or *Reynolds* suits them infinitely better, especially the one with pictures, as they can read *them*. Again, the *Cosmopolitan* has no political or sectarian *clientèle*, and it never can have. It is the organ of no creed, or class, or clique:—

"Pledged to no Party's arbitrary sway,
We follow Truth where'er she leads the way."

Men who look into these columns to find their own pet opinions, traditions, beliefs, proverbs, and catechisms reflected, will always be disappointed. We write to please, or to displease, no one: only to publish what we sincerely believe to be the truth, and nothing but the truth; but not always the *whole truth.* Society would never tolerate *that.* One more question in relation to "business management," touching which we have a whole pigeon-hole full of friendly communications. "How is it," we are asked, "that certain other weekly journals beat you so conspicuously in the advertising department?" We reply to this in one word—"Deadheads." A friend, in order to test this question a few days ago, called on a large number of these "advertisers," and in seven cases out of twelve was informed that their advertisements "were inserted without orders," that they would not pay for them, and that, in many instances, their written request to have the advertisements withdrawn had been utterly disregarded. This fully explains the "discrepancy" which has been so frequently remarked by the friends of the *Cosmopolitan.* We have no space for "deadheads," or for "dummies" to make a show, and serve as "decoy ducks." We trust these explanations will prove satisfactory in answer to the suggestions that have been so frequently made to us during the last eight or nine years; and we will only add, that if any truly cosmopolitan-minded man or woman wishes to become a regular reader and subscriber of the *Cosmopolitan*, there is not a city in Christendom where it cannot be regularly had, at one pound a year, one penny postage included.

"DULCE DOMUM."

> " In happy homes he saw the light
> Of household fires gleam warm and bright."

BUT there was no home for the heaven-seeking youth of Longfellow, neither was there for our poor friend, John Howard Payne, who sang so sweetly of the domestic paradise he never himself enjoyed. And perhaps for that very reason, as it is natural to exaggerate the blessings we do not possess. How sweet the thought of food to a man starving of hunger; how delightful the imaginary glow of fire to one perishing with cold; how charming the dream of home to the homeless! The ideal home is heaven on earth. Alas! that so many households of discord should more nearly represent the *other place*. At this most gracious season of the year, when the hearts of the whole Christian world are softening and expanding under the holy influences of the Ideal One, whom a large portion of mankind has clothed with all divine and human attributes it is possible to conceive, the household becomes a temple consecrated by love, and sanctified by devotion to the loved. Husbands and wives, fathers and mothers, brothers and sisters, are all drawn nearer to each other by the tender cords of family ties and common associations. They feel that they *belong to each other;* and in every happy home "wherein our Saviour's birth is celebrated" there are joys with which the "stranger intermeddleth not." The sacred word *home* belongs alone to the English language, while the ideal home itself is almost exclusively confined to the English-speaking race. We do not say that family affections are stronger among the Anglo-Saxons than among other equally cultivated nations; nor that greater fidelity exists among them between men and women who profess to be, and who ought to be, sacredly and exclusively devoted to each other. In Germany the domestic relations are perhaps as sacred, as true, and as tender as those of any other people. But, 'mid pleasures and palaces though we may roam, be it ever so humble, there is no place like an English home for the development of all the better elements of the human heart, and the culmination of human happiness. A charm from the skies, as our sweet singer says, seems to hallow us there. Without envy, let us congratulate all the dwellers in those sweet homes on this happy Christmas Eve. Since the angels from Heaven sang to the shepherds of

Bethlehem the glorious song of "Peace on earth," there has been no music like the sweet home music, "uttered or unexpressed," which throbs in every heart around the happy fireside to-night. Let all who join in this sacred choir of domestic love and devotion think themselves happy. Let them also give something more than a pitying thought to those houseless and homeless ones who have not where to lay their heads, but who, nevertheless, may lay their poor hearts on the heart of Him who was as poor and as houseless as themselves. Thank God that beautiful Moon, reflecting the light of the Divine Sun, still shines on the darkness of our human night.

THE END.

www.ingramcontent.com/pod-product-compliance
Lightning Source LLC
Chambersburg PA
CBHW030802230426
43667CB00008B/1026